95

Library
Research Guide
to
Sociology

"Library Research Guides" Series

JAMES R. KENNEDY, JR. and
THOMAS G. KIRK, JR., Editors

No. 1   LIBRARY RESEARCH GUIDE TO
                      RELIGION AND THEOLOGY

No. 2   LIBRARY RESEARCH GUIDE TO BIOLOGY

No. 3   LIBRARY RESEARCH GUIDE TO EDUCATION

No. 4   LIBRARY RESEARCH GUIDE TO HISTORY

No. 5   LIBRARY RESEARCH GUIDE TO SOCIOLOGY

Library Research Guide
to
Sociology

Illustrated Search Strategy
and Sources

by
PATRICIA MC MILLAN
Education Librarian,
Founders Memorial Library
Northern Illinois University
and
JAMES R. KENNEDY, JR.
Reference Librarian,
Lilly Library
Earlham College

("Library Research Guides" Series, No. 5)

Pierian Press
ANN ARBOR, MICHIGAN

International Standard Book Numbers: 0-87650-121-8 (cloth);
                                     0-87650-122-6 (paper)
Library of Congress Catalog Card Number: LC 80-83513

Pierian Press, P.O. Box 1808, Ann Arbor, Michigan 48106
Printed in the United States of America

Contents

Preface   vii
Acknowledgements   ix
Introduction   1

1.
Choosing Your Topic.   2
2.
Narrowing Your Topic.   9
3.
Communicating with the Card Catalog.   16
4.
Finding the Best Parts of Books.   19
5.
Evaluating Books.   21
6.
Locating Current Material.   26
7.
Government Documents.   34
8.
Statistical Sources.   36
9.
Dictionaries.   39
10.
Using Guides to the Literature of Sociology.   41
11.
Using Other Libraries.   44
12.
A Last Word and Summary.   47

Appendix 1
Library Knowledge Test.   49
Appendix 2
Basic Reference Sources for Courses in Sociology.   51
Appendix 3
Guidelines for Proceeding.   64
Index of Titles.   67

Preface

Is This the Book You Need?

The answer is yes if you find yourself in one of the following situations:

1. If you are a *college junior or senior majoring in sociology*, you will need to know how to locate appropriate library materials for term papers. This book assumes the card catalog and the *Readers' Guide* are "old friends," but you need to be introduced to the basic reference sources for sociology. If, by some chance, you do *not* know how to use the card catalog and the *Readers' Guide* well, or have not written term papers for other courses that provided good library experience, then read the warning in the last two paragraphs of this preface.

2. If you are a *graduate student in sociology*, you will be writing a number of research papers. This book will guide you to many useful reference sources.

3. If you are a *professor of sociology* or a *reference librarian*, students often ask you for advice on how to find library materials for term papers in sociology. It would be good to be able to recommend a library guide to these students. This is it.

Caveat Lector (Let the Reader Beware)

Do not begin with this book:

1. If you have somehow escaped learning how to use the card catalog and the *Readers' Guide*. Take the five-minute, self-graded test in Appendix 1, in case you wonder how much you know. If you fail the test, save this book until you have read the pages on the card catalog and the *Readers' Guide* in such books as: Margaret G. Cook, *The New Library Key*, 3d ed. (New York: Wilson, 1975); or Ella Aldrich, *Using Books and Libraries*, 5th ed. (Englewood Cliffs, NJ: Prentice-Hall, 1967).

2. If you need to know the general procedures for writing term papers, including notetaking, outlining, and bibliographical forms. Use this book in conjunction with: Kate L. Turabian, *Students' Guide for Writing College Papers*, 3d ed. (Chicago: University of Chicago Press, 1977); or Wilma R. Ebbitt and David R. Ebbitt, *Writer's Guide and Index to English*, 6th ed. (Glenview, IL: Scott, Foresman, 1978).

Acknowledgments

We would especially like to express our appreciation to three people who took time away from their busy schedules to read over our various drafts and make many helpful suggestions. They are Verna Melum Beardsley, a librarian at Northern Illinois University, who for many years was in charge of the library orientation programs and is now retired; Dr. Harley Upchurch, a former Norther Illinois University professor of sociology, who was an avid researcher and library user; and Kenneth R. Muse, a professor of sociology at Earlham College.

Credits for Figures

Thanks are also due to the many publishers cited below who gave their permission to use excerpts from copyrighted works. Without their courtesy this book could not have been the illustrated guide that was intended. Uncopyrighted materials are also cited below in order to make the list of figures complete.

Figure 1:   Pettigrew, Thomas F. "Race Relations; Social-psychological Aspects," *International Encyclopedia of the Social Sciences*, David L. Sills, Editor. New York: Macmillan, 1968, vol. 13, pp. 277, 282; vol. 17, p. 362.

Figure 2:   *Encyclopedia of Social Work*, 17th ed. Washington, DC: National Association of Social Workers, 1977, vol. 2, p. 1,690.

Figure 3:   Faris, Robert E.L. *Handbook of Modern Sociology*. Chicago: Rand McNally, 1964, pp. vii, viii.

Figure 4:   *Annual Review of Sociology*. Palo Alto, CA: Annual Reviews, 1975, vol. 1, pp. 147, 148, 155, 157. Reproduced with permission from the *Annual Review of Sociology*, vol. 1, c1975 by Annual Reviews, Inc.

Figure 5:   Catalog cards.

Figure 6:   Meyer, Jon K. *Bibliography on the Urban Crisis*. Chevy Chase, MD: National Institute of Mental Health, 1969, p. 441.

Figure 7:   Tompkins, Dorothy Campbell, comp. *Poverty in the United States During the Sixties; A Bibliography*. Berkeley, CA: Institute of Governmental Studies, University of California, Berkeley, 1970, p. 394.

Figure 8:   U.S. Social Security Administration, Office of Research and Statistics. *Poverty Studies in the Sixties; A Selected, Annotated Bibliography*. Washington, DC: U.S. Government Printing Office, 1970, table of contents.

Figure 9:   Miller, Elizabeth. *The Negro in America; A Bibliography*. 2d ed. Cambridge, MA: Harvard University Press, 1970, pp. xiv, 132.

Figure 10:   *Blacks in America; Bibliographical Essays*, by James M. McPherson and others. Garden City, NY: Doubleday, 1971, pp. 424, 429, 389, 391, 392.

Figure 11:   Boskin, Joseph. *Urban Racial Violence in the Twentieth Century*. Beverly Hills, CA: Glencoe, 1969, table of contents.

Figure 12:   *Library of Congress Subject Headings*, 9th ed., 2 vols. Washington, DC: Library of Congress, 1980, p. 1,998.

Figure 13:   Catalog card.

Figure 14:   Fogelson, Robert M. *Violence as Protest; A Study of Riots and Ghettos*. Garden City, NY: Doubleday, 1971, table of contents, p. 260.

Figure 15:   *Essay and General Literature Index*, c1970 by The H.W. Wilson Company. Material reproduced by permission of the publisher.

Figure 16:   *Blacks in America; Bibliographical Essays*, by James M. McPherson and others. Garden City, NY: Doubleday, 1971, pp. 391, 392.

Figure 17:   *Book Review Digest*, c1971, 1972 by The H.W. Wilson Company. Material reproduced by permission of the publisher.

Figure 18:   *Book Review Index, 1967 Cumulation*. Detroit: Gale Research, 1968, unpaged.

Figure 19:   American Sociological Association. *1975/1976 Directory of Members*. New York, 1976(?), pp. 434, 647.

Figure 20:   *Biography Index*, c1973, 1974, 1975, 1976, 1977 by The H.W. Wilson Company. Material reproduced by permission of the publisher.

Figure 21:   *Social Sciences & Humanities Index*, c1969 by The H.W. Wilson Company. Material reproduced by permission of the publisher.

Figure 22:   *Sociological Abstracts*, vol. 20 (1972), pp. 2,000, 2,001, 56, 57. Abstracts from *Sociological Abstracts* are reprinted by permission of Sociological Abstracts, Inc., P.O. Box 22206, San Diego, CA 92122.

Figure 23:   *Index to Periodical Articles By and About*

Blacks, cumulated 1960--1970, part II, pp. 555, 556.

Figure 24: *C.R.I.S.; The Combined Retrospective Index Set to Journals in Sociology, 1895--1974*. Washington, DC: Carrollton, 1978, vol. 1, pp. 447, 462, inside of back cover.

Figure 25: *Social Sciences Citation Index*, Citation Index, vol. 2 (1973), column 5,443; Corporate Index, Source Index, vol. 3 (1973), column 1,996; Permuterm Subject Index, vol. 4 (1974), column 6,561; Corporate Index, Source Index, vol. 3 (1974), column 1,874.

Figure 26: *The New York Times Index*, Current Series, vol. 53 (1965), p. 647. c1965 by The New York Times Company. Reprinted by permission.

Figure 27: *Monthly Catalog of United States Government Publications*. Washington, DC: Government Printing Office, 1969, index, p. 524; 1968, index, p. 406; November, 1968, p. 35.

Figure 28: *Statistical Abstract of the United States*. Washington, DC: Government Printing Office, 1973, pp. 1,004, 151.

Figure 29: *American Statistics Index, Annual and Retrospective Edition* (1974), Index, p. 493; Abstracts, p. 1,106.

Figure 30: Hoult, Thomas Ford. *Dictionary of Modern Sociology*. Totowa, NJ: Littlefield, Adams, 1969, p. 262.

Figure 31: Mitchell, Geoffrey. *Dictionary of Sociology*. Chicago: Aldine, 1968, p. 7.

Figure 32: White, Carl M. *Sources of Information in the Social Sciences; A Guide to the Literature*. Chicago: American Library Association, 1973, p. 259. Reprinted by permission of the American Library Association.

Figure 33: Sheehy, Eugene P., comp. *Guide to Reference Books*, 9th ed. Chicago: American Library Association, 1976, pp. 462, 463. Reprinted by permission of the American Library Association.

Figure 34: U.S. Library of Congress. Library of Congress Catalog. *Library of Congress Catalog -- Books: Subjects. A Cumulative List of Works Represented by Library of Congress Printed Cards, 1965--1969*. Ann Arbor, MI: Edwards, 1970, vol. 24, p. 537.

Figure 35: *International Bibliography of Sociology, 1965*. London: Tavistock; Chicago: Aldine, 1966, pp. 270, LXI, 105.

Appendix 1: Library of Congress catalog card; and *Readers' Guide to Periodical Literature*, c1976, 1977 by The H.W. Wilson Company. Material reproduced by permission of the publisher.

Introduction

The history of mankind is little else than a narrative of designs which have failed, and hopes that have been disappointed.
Samuel Johnson, *Works*, vol. 9.

In a sociology class called Social Problems your professor has just announced that one of the course requirements is a fifteen-page term paper. He has left the selection of a specific topic up to you, and he urges you not to wait until the last minute to do your paper. There are some very good reasons for this advice. The selection and subsequent narrowing of a topic is often very time consuming. Discovering the various reference sources available for your topic and how to use them means one or more trips to your library -- not to mention the reading, note taking, outlining, and actual writing and rewriting of the paper. The anticipation of all this may make your mind whirl -- you may even begin to wish you had not signed up for this course! It isn't that you are lazy, but you know from previous experiences that tackling the library and its resources isn't going to be easy, even if you do get started early. Past experiences of fumbling through the card catalog and browsing in the stacks left you bewildered, frustrated, and exhausted!

Well, there is a better way to go about your search. You need to learn an effective search strategy, which may be defined as a systematic way of finding an appropriate term-paper topic and then finding enough important library materials on that topic. The purpose of this guide is to teach basic search strategy and reference sources by working through a sample term-paper topic. The topic that has been chosen is one that is relevant to a sociology course in social problems, but would also be suitable for a course in the sociology of minorities. Excerpts from the basic reference sources relate to the illustrative topic and demonstrate both the search strategy and the use of reference sources. These examples give a concrete demonstration and a general procedure which you can adapt to your own topic. By closely following the steps in this guide you will be guided in carrying out any further term-paper assignments you may encounter. You may see your former frustration turn to confidence and you may even welcome future papers as a chance to pursue your own interests and to be creative.

The difficulty in life is the
choice.
George Moore, *Bending of
the Bough.*

How to Begin to Choose a Topic

When selecting a term-paper topic for your sociology
class, you will want to find a subject that really interests
you. A genuine curiosity about your subject can make your
term-paper assignment rewarding rather than dull and rou-
tine. It will stir your imagination and enliven your writing.
When you have selected such a topic and are equipped with
an effective search strategy and the appropriate reference
sources, you are on your way to a successful paper.

Perhaps your curiosity has been hooked by the class
discussion as to *why* there is so much violence in America,
especially in the 1960s which has been called one of the
most violent decades in the entire history of our country.
The violence that flourised in the 1960s took many forms.
Some of these were: war (Vietnam), a significant increase
of the crimes of murder, theft, and rape; political assassinations (the Kennedys and King); hijacking; rioting in our
universities, streets, and prisons; and widespread charges of
police brutality. You realize right away that you can't
adequately cover *all* of these various forms of violence in a
fifteen--page paper. Therefore you decide to study a specific
kind of violence. Maybe you are concerned about the plight
of Black Americans and therefore decide you would like to
study racial violence in the United States. This interest may
have been aroused by reading the following sentence: "We
began, after all, as a people who killed red men and en-
slaved black men." This quote appears on page 31 of Arthur
Schlesinger, Jr.'s *Violence: America in the Sixties* (1968).

Why Look for Authoritative Summarizing Discussions?

Your first step should be to find one or more authoritative summarizing discussions of your topic. Perhaps you are
thinking: "Why can't I go straight to the card catalog, select
a few books on racial violence, and be through with my
library research?" This shortcut to library research, although
very popular, has serious weaknesses. When you base a term
paper on a few randomly chosen books, you run the danger
of repeating any biases or errors the authors may have had.
Another weakness of this shortcut approach is that it tends
to commit you too soon to a topic or subtopic. It does not
let you shop around. To avoid difficulties and to get off
to a good start, look for summarizing articles to read. Summaries allow you to survey the forest before you focus on a
tree or a single leaf of the tree. A broader perspective will
help you avoid the errors caused by a limited outlook. At
the same time the summaries let you see how a subject has
been subdivided, and help you focus on one of its subdivisions. If the summaries fail to stimulate your curiosity
in the topic, then you can switch to another topic without
much loss of time. Summaries have all these benefits, and
they take only a few minutes to consult.

Where to Find Summarizing Discussions

These summarizing discussions can be found in certain
encyclopedias, in textbooks, and by asking your reference
librarian. For the field of sociology the best encyclopedia
to consult is the *International Encyclopedia of the Social
Sciences*, 17 vols. (New York: Macmillan, 1968). Over 500
of the world's most capable social scientists have contributed articles to this work. This set represents the social sciences in the 1960s and it reflects the development and recent
rapid expansion in the field. The articles do not stress facts
but concepts and present the major principles, theories, and
methods in the disciplines of anthropology, economics,
geography, history, law, political science, psychiatry, psychology, sociology, and statistics. The contributors were
asked to emphasize the analytical and comparative aspects
of a topic rather than the historical and descriptive material
treated in the earlier *Encyclopedia of the Social Sciences*,
15 vols. (New York: Macmillan, 1930--34). At the end of
each article is a bibliography listing additional readings,
some of which may be very useful. The separate index volume is the place to begin. For example, let's say that you
take the index volume and look at the subject heading,
"race relations," which is in bold print. As FIGURE 1
shows, this has a subdivision, "social-psychological aspects."
Perhaps this will be just the summarizing article you need.

You note, as FIGURE 1 shows, that social scientists
view race relations as a subdivision of intergroup relations.
The article goes on to identify and discuss concepts and
principles helpful in understanding relations between racial
groups. This is done in only five pages, which are signed
by Thomas F. Pettigrew, a prominent social psychologist at
Harvard University. The bibliography of additional readings,
excerpted in FIGURE 1, may be useful to you for further
information on this topic.

Another source of summarizing articles is the *Encyclopedia of Social Work*, 17th ed., 2 vols. (Washington, DC:
National Association of Social Workers, 1977). The various

"The problem of the Twentieth Century," wrote W. E. B. DuBois prophetically in 1903, "is the problem of the color line." And, to be sure, together with related concerns it is the problem of the twentieth century. In an era of rising expectations, "the color line" is of...

...᷄ᵤᵤ...᷄ᵤᵤ colonialism to poverty and war.

Important as it is, however, social scientists typically view race relations (the social interactions between any two or more socially or biologically defined "races") as merely a particularly potent special case of intergroup relations (the social interactions between any two or more identifiable...

...phenomena progresses.

Broadly speaking, all intergroup relations are conditioned by four interrelated classes of factors: historical, sociocultural, individual, and situational (adapted from Allport 1954). The first set relates

...increasingly

...increasingly greater ef-

...participants. This possibility is of

...relevance to such intergroup processes as India's efforts to end caste discrimination and the United States' efforts to end racial segregation.

THOMAS F. PETTIGREW

BIBLIOGRAPHY

ADORNO, THEODOR W. et al. 1950 *The Authoritar[ian] Per-sonality.* American Jewish Committee, Social [Stu]dies Series, No. 3. New York: Harper.

ALLPORT, GORDON W. 1954 *The Nature of Prej[udice.]* Reading, Mass.: Addison-Wesley. → A[ ] perback edition was published [ ]

BATTACCHI, MARCO W. 19[ ] *nella stru[ ]* l[ ]

LEE, ALFRED M.; and HUMPHREY, NORMAN D. 1943 *Race Riot.* New York: Dryden.

LOHMAN, J. D.; and REITZES, D. C. 1952 A Note on Race Relations in Mass Society. *American Journal of Sociology* 58, no. 3:240–246.

OKLAHOMA, UNIVERSITY OF, INSTITUTE OF GROUP RELA-TIONS 1961 *Intergroup Conflict and Cooperation: The Robbers Cave Experiment,* by Muzafer Sherif et al. Norman, Okla.: University Book Exchange.

PATAI, RAPHAEL 1953 *Israel Between East and West: A Study in Human Relations.* Philadelphia: Jewish Publication Society of America.

PETTIGREW, THOMAS F. 1964 *A Pro[ ]* American. Princeton, N[ ]

PETTIGREW, THO[ ] T[ ]

INDEX

RACE RELATIONS 13:269–282

WORLD PERSPECTIVES 13:269–277
SOCIAL-PSYCHOLOGICAL ASPECTS 13:277–282

civil disobedience 2:480, 482
constitutional law: civil rights 3:315
DuBois, W. E. B. 4:305
ethnic groups 5:167
Fanon, Frantz 5:326
Frazier, E. Franklin 5:553
Johnson, Charles S. 8:262
literature: political fiction 9:433
marriage: family formation 10:6
police 12:176
social movements 14:450

Figure 1. International Encyclopedia of the Social Sciences

topics in this work link social problems and social work with social theories, as well as the societal context in which problems occur. At the end of each article is a bibliography.

When you turn to the index in the back you find no listings under the heading "riots," but, as FIGURE 2 shows, when you look under the heading "Minorities: Blacks," you find the subdivision "in central cities" which leads to several useful pages. To use an index effectively you may have to try several headings.

..., 190;
..., 933; research
...-J2; as rural people, 1229-
...ermination, 949–50; social services,
...JU–51; welfare services expenditures for, 455
MINORITIES: ASIAN AMERICANS, **953–60;** barriers to delivery and utilization of services, 958; culturally relevant social services, 958–59; current situation, 954–56; future developments, 959–60; in rural areas, 1229; social services, 956–57
MINORITIES: BLACKS, **960–66;** arrest rates among, 943; average age of black women, 962; black women participation of, in labor force, 751–52; in central cities, 313, 314, 316–17, 961; civil rights of, 181–85; current sociodemographic characteristics, 961–62; disaster relief for, 284; and economic theory of labor force behavior, 751–52; education of, 942, 943, 962; effects of family planning on fertility of black women, 415; employment for, 316–17, 962; family breakdown among, 376–77; government programs, 964–65; health care for, 526, 527, 533; health status of, 943–44; historical background, 960–61; history of programs to aid, 1507–8; housing conditions of, 402, 644; income of, 402, 700, 777–78, 932, 940–42, 962; indicators of well-being, 962; infant mortality among, 535, 873, 962; manpower development programs for, 791; migration from the South, 915–17; need for control of services, 966; need for income maintenance policy, 965–66; in 1960s civil disorders, 945; number of, 931, 961; number of working women, 360; occupational mobility of, 798–801; prematurity among, 873; relocation of, 664–65; rural, 1229–30; self-help institutions and organizations, 962–64; single-parent families among, 358, 401; subemployment among, 809; unemployment among, 755–5? 8, 940–42; withdrawing fro·· ·
See also Race
MINORI⊤!⊤·

Figure 2. Encyclopedia of Social Work

Using Handbooks

Sometimes a handbook will provide a worthwhile summarizing article. A handbook is literally a small book which can be held in the hand and many are like one-volume encyclopedias because they treat broad subjects in brief fashion. Others provide odd bits of information about a variety of topics.

The field of sociology has several excellent handbooks.

The *Handbook of Modern Sociology*, edited by Robert E.L. Faris (Chicago: Rand McNally, 1964), aims to summarize all the major ares of modern sociology and indicate how some of the areas are related to each other. The table of contents, shown in FIGURE 3, reports there is a 44--page chapter entitled "race and ethnic relations." At the end of this and the other chapters there are extensive bibliographies.

The Handbook of Social Psychology, edited by Gardner Lindzey and Elliot Aronson, 2d ed., 5 vols. (Reading, MA: Addison-Wesley, 1968--69) is another useful handbook. Each volume deals with a different aspect of sociology and its chapters are followed by extensive bibliographies. Volume five is subtitled "Applied Social Psychology" and has a 76-page chapter entitled "Prejudice and Ethnic Relations."

The *Handbook of Socialization Theory and Research*, edited by David A. Goslin, (Chicago: Rand McNally, 1969), consists of a collection of theoretical essays related to the general area of socialization. This work is aimed at both graduate students and experienced researchers. Its chapter entitled "Socialization of American Minority Peoples" is 38 pages long.

Using Annual Reviews

Annual reviews are yearly volumes that discuss developments within a subject area, and they are still another place to find a summarizing article. They provide a time-saving way to keep up with a field or to get an overview of a field. The contributing writers are usually leading authorities, and they provide extensive bibliographies.

For sociologists the most useful annual review is the *Annual Review of Sociology* (Palo Alto, CA: Annual Reviews, 1975--). Volume one, 1975, has sixteen bibliographic essays, including a 40-page one, "Race and Ethnic Relations," by Robin M. Williams, Jr., a sociology professor at Cornell. This volume has no index, but this essay is carefully outlined. Section "III 9" is entitled "Civil Disorders, Riots, or Rebellions." As FIGURE 4 shows, Williams wrote that "Another feature of recent study of violent conflict has been the increased use of complex multivariate models to aid in seeking causal inferences. Both are exemplified in the work of Spilerman (1970; 1971, a, b) Jiobu (1971, 1974) and Downes (1970) on urban civil disorders . . . " Each of the authors and dates refers to a publication cited at the end of the chapter. For example, FIGURE 4 shows that "Downes (1970)" refers to "Downes, B.T. 1970. A critical reexamination of the social and political characteristics of riot cities. *Soc. Sci. Quart.* 51:349--60."

The following three annual reviews of use to sociologists started publication before 1975: *Annual Review of Anthropology* (Palo Alto, CA: Annual Reviews, 1972--); its predecessor, *Biennial Review of Anthropology* (Stanford, CA: Stanford University Press, 1959–71); and *Annual Review of Psychology* (Palo Alto, CA: Annual Reviews, 1950--). Most of their bibliographic essays are for anthropologists and psychologists, but they are worth investigating

Table of Contents

1. THE DISCIPLINE OF SOCIOLOGY   1
   Robert E. L. Faris

2. SOCIAL ORGANIZATION AND THE ECOSYSTEM   37
   Otis Dudley Duncan

3. POPULATION AND SOCIETY   83
   Irene B. Taeuber

4. THE RURAL-URBAN DIMENSION IN PREINDUSTRIAL, TRAN-
   SITIONAL, AND INDUSTRIAL SOCIETIES   127
   Gideon Sjoberg

5. LABOR FORCE   161
   Philip M. Hauser

6. POSITION AND BEHAVIOR PATTERNS OF YO~   272
   David Matza

7. INTE~~~   ~r HEALTH AND ILLNESS   310
            ~~~AM

10. SOCIAL EFFECTS OF MASS COMMUNICATION   349
    Otto N. Larsen

11. COLLECTIVE BEHAVIOR   382
    Ralph H. Turner

12. SOCIAL MOVEMENTS   426
    Lewis M. Killian

13. NORMS, VALUES, AND SANCTIONS   456
    Judith Blake and Kingsley Davis

14. THEORY OF ORGANIZATIONS   485
    W. Richard Scott

15. SOCIAL DIFFERENTIATION   530
    Kaare Svalastoga

16. RACE AND ETHNIC RELATIONS   ~~~
    Frank R. Westie

17. INDUSTRIAL RELATIONS
    Edward Gross

18. ~~~

Figure 3. Handbook of Modern Sociology

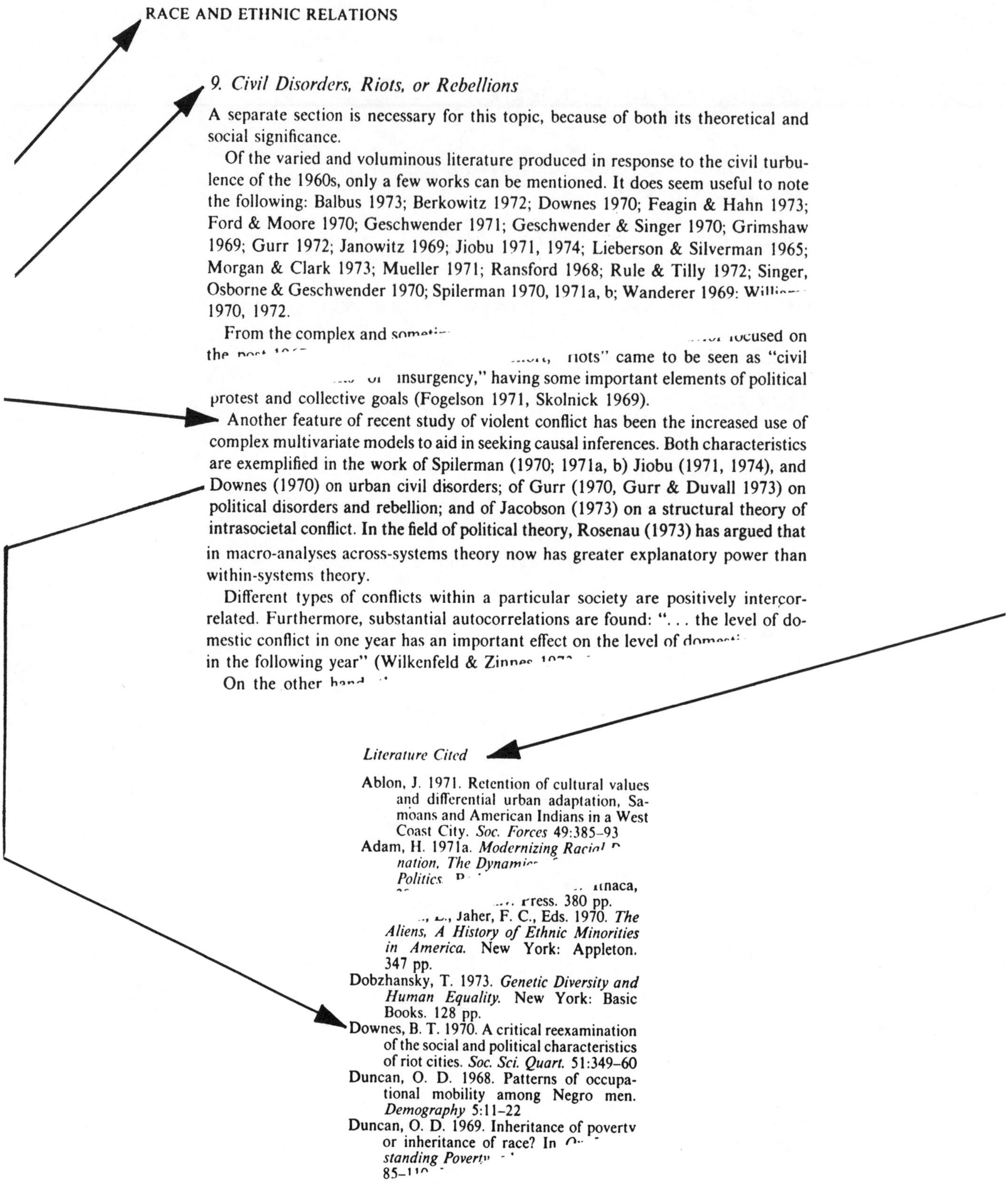

9. Civil Disorders, Riots, or Rebellions

A separate section is necessary for this topic, because of both its theoretical and social significance.

Of the varied and voluminous literature produced in response to the civil turbulence of the 1960s, only a few works can be mentioned. It does seem useful to note the following: Balbus 1973; Berkowitz 1972; Downes 1970; Feagin & Hahn 1973; Ford & Moore 1970; Geschwender 1971; Geschwender & Singer 1970; Grimshaw 1969; Gurr 1972; Janowitz 1969; Jiobu 1971, 1974; Lieberson & Silverman 1965; Morgan & Clark 1973; Mueller 1971; Ransford 1968; Rule & Tilly 1972; Singer, Osborne & Geschwender 1970; Spilerman 1970, 1971a, b; Wanderer 1969; Willi--- 1970, 1972.

From the complex and somet--- ... ...ocused on the post 196- ...., riots" came to be seen as "civil ... or insurgency," having some important elements of political protest and collective goals (Fogelson 1971, Skolnick 1969).

Another feature of recent study of violent conflict has been the increased use of complex multivariate models to aid in seeking causal inferences. Both characteristics are exemplified in the work of Spilerman (1970; 1971a, b) Jiobu (1971, 1974), and Downes (1970) on urban civil disorders; of Gurr (1970, Gurr & Duvall 1973) on political disorders and rebellion; and of Jacobson (1973) on a structural theory of intrasocietal conflict. In the field of political theory, Rosenau (1973) has argued that in macro-analyses across-systems theory now has greater explanatory power than within-systems theory.

Different types of conflicts within a particular society are positively intercorrelated. Furthermore, substantial autocorrelations are found: "... the level of domestic conflict in one year has an important effect on the level of domesti- in the following year" (Wilkenfeld & Zinnes 107- -

On the other hand ---

Literature Cited

Ablon, J. 1971. Retention of cultural values and differential urban adaptation, Samoans and American Indians in a West Coast City. *Soc. Forces* 49:385–93

Adam, H. 1971a. *Modernizing Racir- ᴺ nation, The Dynamic- Politics.* ᴾ - ... ...naca, ... rress. 380 pp.

..., ᴸ., Jaher, F. C., Eds. 1970. *The Aliens, A History of Ethnic Minorities in America.* New York: Appleton. 347 pp.

Dobzhansky, T. 1973. *Genetic Diversity and Human Equality.* New York: Basic Books. 128 pp.

Downes, B. T. 1970. A critical reexamination of the social and political characteristics of riot cities. *Soc. Sci. Quart.* 51:349–60

Duncan, O. D. 1968. Patterns of occupational mobility among Negro men. *Demography* 5:11–22

Duncan, O. D. 1969. Inheritance of poverty or inheritance of race? In ᴼ-- ˙ standing Povert~ - ˙ 85–11ᴼ - ˙

Figure 4. Annual Review of Sociology

because anthropology is closely related to sociology and social psychology is a branch of psychology. For example, the 1977 volume of the *Annual Review of Psychology* has an essay entitled "Social and Community Interventions."

Using Textbooks and Reserve Books

Textbooks and reserve books are often good sources in which to find authoritative summaries of a topic. If your text does not provide an adequate summary of your tenta-

tively chosen topic, try the books placed on reserve by your professor. He has placed certain books on reserve because he regards them as authoritative.

To locate other textbooks besides your own, you can check the card catalog of the library. Most libraries will have *some* textbooks but not an extensive collection of them. It is the college or university bookstore which specializes in textbooks. However, the library does have many introductory and supplementary materials. Take your own text, look in the card catalog under the author's name and try to find the title. Then note the subject heading or headings

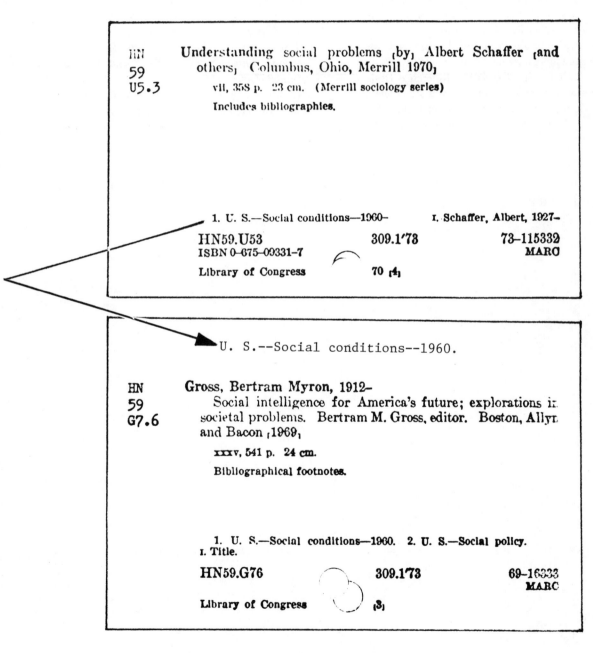

Figure 5. Catalog Cards

which are printed at the bottom of the card, as shown in FIGURE 5. These headings can be looked up in the card catalog in order to see what similar books the library owns.

For example, let's say that your textbook is *Understanding Social Problems* by Albert Schaffer. Going to the card catalog, you look under the title and find the catalog card shown in FIGURE 5. At the bottom of the card the subject headings for this book is: "U.S. -- Social Conditions -- 1960-- ." As FIGURE 5 shows, you can find similar books under this heading. If your textbook is not listed in the card catalog, you may need to ask your reference librarian to find the appropriate subject headings.

It is possible, even after exploring encyclopedias, handbooks, annual reviews, textbooks, and reserve books, that you will not be able to find the summaries you need. Don't give up though. Ask your reference librarian for help again. The librarian is hired especially to help students use the library. A graduate degree in library science has prepared the librarian to advise students on reference sources. Thus, if you have a problem, don't be shy. Go to the Reference Desk. Ask your question as precisely as you can and state where you have already looked. You may be led to encyclopedias you never heard of, or you may be shown how to use the subject heading book, which will be described in Chapter 3. However, the librarian may conclude that the library does not have the summaries and resources you need, and therefore recommend that you change your topic. It is much better to change a dead end topic early, before you have invested too much time in it. In any case, it is wise to talk early and often to your librarian, a term-paper writer's best friend.

Summary

1. Choose a topic which really interests you.
2. Begin your library research by reading summarizing discussions.
3. These summarizing discussions may be found in certain encyclopedias, handbooks, annual reviews, textbooks, or reserve books. Of special importance are the *International Encyclopedia of the Social Sciences* and the *Annual Review of Sociology*.
4. Whenever you have difficulty, ask for help. Your reference librarian is there primarily to help you.

A man is rich in proportion
to the things he can afford to
let alone.
Henry David Thoreau.

Why Narrow Your Topic

As pointed out above, the topic with which you begin will often need to be narrowed, unless your professor states otherwise. There are several good reasons for this. Remember, you are only writing a term paper, not a whole book. Most topics, as originally chosen, are topics on which whole books have been written. For example, a beginning topic, such as "Race Relations in Urban America," is so broad that many books have been written about it. Time does not permit you to write a book; that would require months of library research. You will probably be surprised to find, when you begin digging into reference sources, that the library has a great deal of information on your topic. When this is so, you will automatically see the need to narrow your topic. As you narrow your topic, you will be glad to see your required reading has been decreased.

How to Narrow Your Topic: Encyclopedias

Perhaps you are thinking: "Just how can I go about narrowing my topic?" Well, there are several ways you can do the job. First, you can use the same encyclopedias, handbooks, annual reviews, textbooks, and reserve books mentioned earlier for their summaries, and see how they subdivide your topic. One of the subdivisions may be an appropriate topic.

For example, perhaps you used *The Negro Almanac* compiled by Harry A. Ploski and Roscoe C. Brown (New York: Bellwether, 1967). This specialized handbook covers a wide range of topics and gives summaries of current information on the main aspects of Black life in America; it includes statistical tables, and has an author and subject index. Consulting the index of *The Negro Almanac*, you find under the heading "riots" a listing of individual cities where

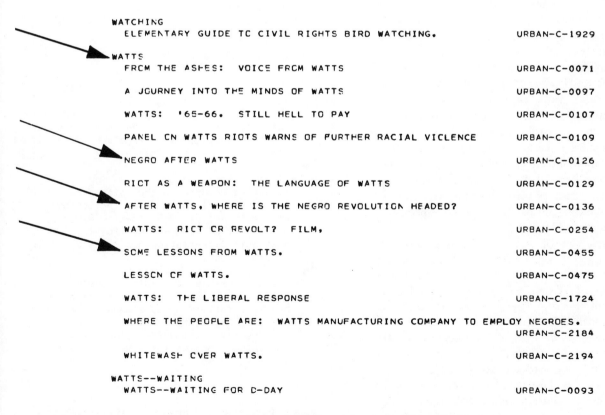

Figure 6. Bibliography on the Urban Crisis

riots occurred. You may want to focus on a particular riot that occurred in a given city. Let's say that you turn to page 41 which describes the Watts Riot in Los Angeles in 1965, a significant riot which claimed thirty-five lives and resulted in multi-million dollar damage. You may decide to devote your term paper to this particular riot.

But, as you use various reference sources, you will find that there is a great deal written just on this one riot. This realization will lead you, in time, to narrow your topic further, perhaps by focusing on the "causes of the riot," a subtopic of the *Negro Almanac*'s article on the Los Angeles riot. You might even focus on one of the seven causes listed, such as "police brutality."

Bibliographies

Second, you can use bibliographies in order to select a viable subtopic. "Bibliography" is the word for a list of writings that are selected and arranged in order to show some relationship to each other. There are several kinds of bibliographies. The general bibliography is not limited to one subject, whereas the subject bibliography covers only one subject. National or regional bibliographies include material related to one country or to one region. Trade bibliographies are prepared for the book trade and supply information needed for buying and selling books.

A bibliography may be comprehensive and attempt to include all works of a particular kind, or it may be selective and contain only part of the works. It may be descriptive and have a brief comment on each book listed; or it may be evaluative, with critical comments. It could be both descriptive and evaluative.

Subject bibliographies are useful anytime you need writings on a subject. They locate material on a subject and provide the author's name, complete title of the work, place of publication, publisher, date of publication, edition, and perhaps number of pages. If annotated, they indicate the scope of the subject and the manner in which it is treated. If the annotations are critical and evaluative, they comment upon the usefulness of the publication. Bibliographies point out material, such as parts of books, which cannot be analyzed in the card catalog. As you might expect, they can save much time in a literature search.

For your topic you will want to find some good subject bibliographies. Since they are more specialized, you may not know which ones to consult. Here again your reference librarian can suggest general and specific subject bibliographies which will be useful to you. A very useful bibliography for your sociological study of racial riots is Jon K. Meyer's *Bibliography on the Urban Crisis* (Chevy Chase, MD: National Institute of Mental Health, 1969). This bibliography, found in the card catalog under the subject heading "Violence -- U.S. -- Bibliography," lists material on the causes, effects, and responses to urban civil disorders. Emphasis has been placed on the years between 1954 and 1968 but earlier material has also been included. There are several items listed on Watts in the index shown in FIGURE 6. For example, the works entitled "Negro After Watts," "After Watts, Where Is the Negro Revolution Heading?" and "Some Lessons from Watts," suggest that you might wish to concentrate on the results of the Watts Riot.

Two bibliographies listing materials on various aspects of poverty in the sixties that could be useful for your topic are: Dorothy Tompkins' *Poverty in the United States During the Sixties; A Bibliography* (Berkeley, CA: Institute of Governmental Studies, University of California, 1970) and *Poverty Studies in the Sixties; A Selected, Annotated Bibliography* by the Social Security Administration, Office of Research and Statistics (Washington, DC: U.S. Government Printing Office, 1970). You might pursue the topic of poverty in the Watts area and concentrate on the constructive economic measures. In this case you would use Tompkins' bibliography, as shown in FIGURE 7. The table of con-

---

programs.
Conference Bulletin 69: 21, Fall 1965.

A self-help program stirs a Negro slum. Business Week, March 25, 1967: 67-68+ 7428
Concerning Operation Bootstrap, in Watts.

Stadum, Edward M.
A new approach to black business. San Francisco Business 4: 37-38+

National
Service. Records Management Division. Region 9, San Francisco
Study of management-organization and administrative practices of the Economic Opportunity Council of San Francisco. v.p. (mim) (preliminary draft) March 1967 7432

Williams, William J.
Attacking poverty in the Watts area: small business development under the Economic Opportunity Act of 1964. Thesis (D.P.A.), University of Southern California, 1966
Abstract: Dissertation Abstracts 27: 1430A, November 1966. 7433

Wolcott, Robert B. and Nuffer, David
Helping an infant black firm--volunteer public relations gives a hand to new enterprise in the Watts area. 7434
Concerning Community Pride, Inc.
Reprinted: Congressional Record, June 23, 1969: E5147-48.

Figure 7. Poverty in the United States During the Sixties; A Bibliography

tents of the bibliography entitled *Poverty Studies in the Sixties* presents many aspects of poverty, as shown in FIGURE 8. One of the subdivisions, such as "discrimination against minorities" or "federal and related antipoverty programs," might be useful to a study of the Watts riot.

Your reference librarian may suggest that you should consult some of the many bibliographies of writings on Blacks. Two specialized bibliographies are Elizabeth Miller's *The Negro in America; A Bibliography*, 2d ed. (Cambridge, MA: Harvard University Press, 1970); and *Blacks in America; Bibliographical Essays*, by James M. McPherson and others (Garden City, NY: Doubleday, 1971). The former is a fairly recent selective bibliography citing contemporary writings about Blacks. Some of the books and articles included in this source are briefly annotated. *Blacks in America*, by McPherson, combines narration with bibliography in a chronological and topical framework that provides an up-to-date guide to Afro-American history and culture. It utilizes an interdisciplinary approach and many of the topics are subdivided. Each major topic is introduced by one or more paragraphs summarizing the factual data and interpretive questions involved in the study, followed by a discussion of the major books, articles, and primary sources cited. Both bibliographies are arranged by subject but only *Blacks in*

CONTENTS

General Background... 1
    Collections of Articles
    Present Income Transfers

The Concept of Poverty..................................... 7
    Defining and Measuring
    Philosophy of Antipoverty Action
    Economic Growth

Some Significant Aspects of Poverty....................... 23
    Discrimination Against Minorities
    Culture and Subcultures
    Poverty Among the Aged

Health and Poverty.. 39

Poverty and the Law....................................... 41

Reduction of Selected Deprivations....................... 45
    Employment and Earnings
    Rural and Regional Poverty
    Education for the Disadvantaged

Urban Housing and Development............................. 63

Legislation... 73
    Area and Regional Redevelopment
    Economic Opportunity Act
    Education: Elementary and Secondary, and Vocational
    Food Stamps
    Housing and Urban Legislation
    Manpower Development and Training
    Migratory Farm Labor
    Social Security and Welfare

Federal and Related Antipoverty Programs.................. 79
    Program Descriptions
    Appraisal and Evaluation of Antipoverty Programs

Alternative or Supplementary Programs.................... 103
    Public Income Maintenance Programs
    Governmental Allowances and Income Guarantees

Author Index... 121

Figure 8. Poverty Studies in the Sixties; A Selected, Annotated Bibliography

America has a subject index.

To use *The Negro in America* turn to its table of contents. FIGURE 9 shows that the subject heading "urban problems" has a subheading "race violence and riots" which looks promising. Turning to page 132, shown in FIGURE 9, you will find several books and articles on Watts.

To use *Blacks in America*, start with its index, as shown in FIGURE 10. By cross checking the pages cited under "Riots" and under "Watts district, Los Angeles," you find that pages 389 and 391--392 deal with the Watts riot. Pages 391 and 392 discuss several books, including Paul Bullock's *Watts: The Aftermath . . .* which "affords an invaluable perspective on why and how Watts happened." This is the kind of helpful comment that you get from bibliographic essays.

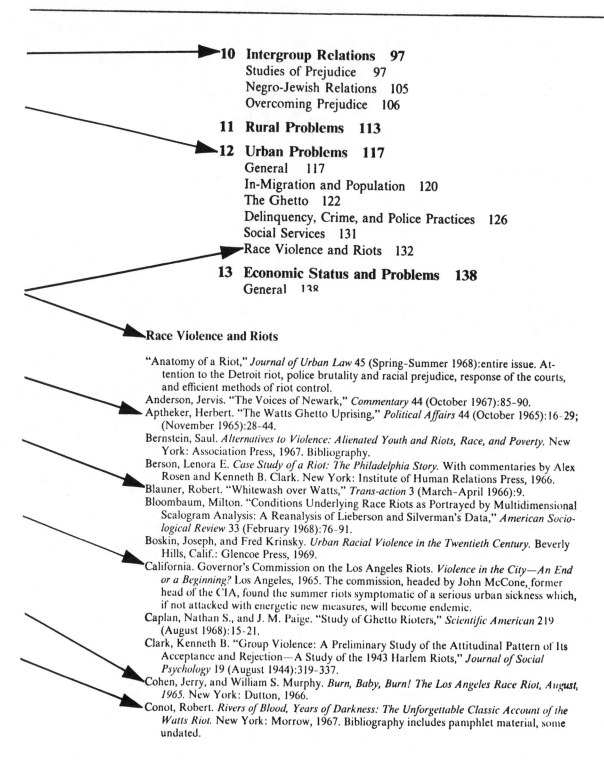

10 Intergroup Relations 97
Studies of Prejudice 97
Negro-Jewish Relations 105
Overcoming Prejudice 106

11 Rural Problems 113

12 Urban Problems 117
General 117
In-Migration and Population 120
The Ghetto 122
Delinquency, Crime, and Police Practices 126
Social Services 131
Race Violence and Riots 132

13 Economic Status and Problems 138
General 138

Race Violence and Riots

"Anatomy of a Riot," *Journal of Urban Law* 45 (Spring-Summer 1968):entire issue. Attention to the Detroit riot, police brutality and racial prejudice, response of the courts, and efficient methods of riot control.

Anderson, Jervis. "The Voices of Newark," *Commentary* 44 (October 1967):85-90.

Aptheker, Herbert. "The Watts Ghetto Uprising," *Political Affairs* 44 (October 1965):16-29; (November 1965):28-44.

Bernstein, Saul. *Alternatives to Violence: Alienated Youth and Riots, Race, and Poverty.* New York: Association Press, 1967. Bibliography.

Berson, Lenora E. *Case Study of a Riot: The Philadelphia Story.* With commentaries by Alex Rosen and Kenneth B. Clark. New York: Institute of Human Relations Press, 1966.

Blauner, Robert. "Whitewash over Watts," *Trans-action* 3 (March–April 1966):9.

Bloombaum, Milton. "Conditions Underlying Race Riots as Portrayed by Multidimensional Scalogram Analysis: A Reanalysis of Lieberson and Silverman's Data," *American Sociological Review* 33 (February 1968):76-91.

Boskin, Joseph, and Fred Krinsky. *Urban Racial Violence in the Twentieth Century.* Beverly Hills, Calif.: Glencoe Press, 1969.

California. Governor's Commission on the Los Angeles Riots. *Violence in the City—An End or a Beginning?* Los Angeles, 1965. The commission, headed by John McCone, former head of the CIA, found the summer riots symptomatic of a serious urban sickness which, if not attacked with energetic new measures, will become endemic.

Caplan, Nathan S., and J. M. Paige. "Study of Ghetto Rioters," *Scientific American* 219 (August 1968):15-21.

Clark, Kenneth B. "Group Violence: A Preliminary Study of the Attitudinal Pattern of Its Acceptance and Rejection—A Study of the 1943 Harlem Riots," *Journal of Social Psychology* 19 (August 1944):319-337.

Cohen, Jerry, and William S. Murphy. *Burn, Baby, Burn! The Los Angeles Race Riot, August, 1965.* New York: Dutton, 1966.

Conot, Robert. *Rivers of Blood, Years of Darkness: The Unforgettable Classic Account of the Watts Riot.* New York: Morrow, 1967. Bibliography includes pamphlet material, some undated.

Figure 9. The Negro in America; A Bibliography

13. Urban Racial Violence: The 1960s

A decade of civil rights activity accomplished substantial change in the legal status of black men in America but very little change in the deep-rooted social and economic ills of the black ghetto. Long-simmering frustrations and grievances...

police... ...over the period 1863–1968,

...chen, ed., *Race Riots in Black and White* (Englewood Cliffs, N.J., 1970).*

There is already a voluminous literature analyzing the riot phenomenon and chronicling outbreaks in various cities. Harlem is treated in Fred C. Shapiro and James W. Sullivan, *Race Riots: New York, 1964* (New York, 1964). Lenora E. Berson, *Case Study of a Riot: The Philadelphia Story* (New York, 1966), is a pamphlet on the 1964 outbreak in that city. Among the individual riots, Watts has received the most intensive coverage to date. Robert E. Conot gives what is probably the best narrative account of Watts by an outsider in *Rivers of Blood, Years of Darkness* (Toronto, Ont., 1967),* but Jerry Cohen and William S. Murphy, *Burn, Baby, Burn! The Los Angeles Race Riot, August, 1965* (New York, 1966), and Spencer Crump, *Black Riot in Los Angeles: The Story of the Watts Tragedy* (Los Angeles, 1966), should also be consulted. Paul Bullock, ed., *Watts: The Aftermath; An Inside View of the Ghetto by the People of Watts* (New York, 1970),* affords an invaluable perspective on why and how Watts happened. Nathan Cohen, ed., *The Los Angeles Riots: A Socio-Psychological Study* (New York, 1970), is extremely thorough and informative. See also David O. Sears and T. M. Tomlinson, "Riot Ideology in Los Angeles: A Study of Negro Attitudes," SSQ, XLIX (Dec. 1968), 485–503, which also appears as ch. 30 of Glenn and Bonjean, eds., *Blacks in the United States*, cited above; Anthony Oberschall, "The Los Angeles Riot of August 1965," *Social Problems*, XV (Winter 1968), 322–41; H. Edward Ransford, "Isolation, Powerlessness, and Violence: A Study of Attitudes and Participation in the Watts Riot." AJS LXXIII... 1968), 581–91;** and "W..."

M... ...al report of the ...on on the Los Angeles Riots (the McCone Commission), *Violence in the City—An End or a Beginning?* (Los Angeles, 1965), has been the subject of much criticism; for a sample of views, see Paul Jacobs, *Prelude to Riot: A View of Urban America from the Bottom* (New York, 1967),* a detailed analysis of black grievances in Los Angeles; Robert M. Fogelson, "White on Black: A Critique of the McCone Commission Report on the Los Angeles Riots," PSQ, LXXXII (Sept. 1967), 337–67;** Bayard Rustin, "The Watts 'Manifesto' and the McCone Report," *Commentary*, XLI (Mar. 1966), 29–35; and Robert Blauner, "Whitewash over Watts," *Trans-action*, III (Mar.–Apr. 1966), 9.

There is an account of th...

INDEX

Richey, Elinor, 359–60
Riddleberger, Patrick W., 130
Riesman, David, 165, 214, 335, 385
Riley, Clayton, 280, 282
Riots, 96, 138–42, 152, 170; anti-abolitionist, 91–92; draft, 113; ghetto, 191, 194–97, 354, 389–96; military, 235; poverty and, 345, 346, 350; the press and, 295
Rippy, J. Fred, 172
Risher, Howard W., Jr., 346
Rivkin, Malcolm D., 359
Roach, Jack L., 403
Roach...

...son, Forbes, 273
Watson, Tom, 137
Watters, Pat, 375
Watts, Lewis G., 359
Watts district, Los Angeles, 330, 389, 391–92
WAVES, 234
Wax, Darold D., 43, 45
Weales, Gerald C., 261, 278, 282–83, 284
Weatherford, Willis D., 79, 209
Weatherly, Tom, 245
Weaver, John D...

You won't get such comments from most bibliographies or from the card catalog. It is just what you want to know if you are focusing on the causes of the Watts riot.

The Card Catalog

A *third* way to narrow your topic is provided by the card catalog. For example, "Race" is a very broad subject heading. A narrower subject heading would be "Riots -- U.S." and a still narrower heading would be for specific riots occurring in individual cities, such as "Los Angeles -- Riots, 1965." How to arrive at these headings will be discussed in the next chapter.

Browsing

Yet a *fourth* way to "pare down" a topic is to go to the shelves and examine the tables of contents and indexes of books found in the card catalog under the most relevant subject headings mentioned above. For example, when you use the card catalog, you may find several books that look very promising. You would then copy the call numbers and go to the stacks. Browsing through the appropriate section of the stacks, you come across a book by Joseph Boskin, entitled *Urban Racial Violence in the Twentieth Century* (1969). This work looks like it might be just what you need. When you scan the table of contents, shown in Figure 11, you see

CONTENTS

Part One: Race Riots

1. Race Prejudice: The Fear of R~~

~~ ~~ ~~, Illinois Race Riot of 1908,
James L. Crouthamel, 8

2. World War I: The Effect of Job Competition 21

East Saint Louis (1917), *24*
The Riot of Washington, D.C. (1919), *28*
The Chicago Riot (1919), *30*

3. World War II: The In~~

Part Two: Protest Riots

5. The Causes of Protest Riots in the 1960's   65

The Civil Rights Commission Report ~~
"An Ancient ~~ ~~ying Force (1966),
~~erick J. Hacker, M.D., with Aljean Harmetz, 87*

6. Four Major Protest Riots: Harlem, Watts, Newark, Detroit   93

A Nation of Two Societies (1968), *95*
Harlem: Hatred in the Streets (1964), *100*
The Watts Manifesto (1965), *Bayard Rustin, 109*
Newark: On the Salt Marshes of the Passaic River (1968), *116*
An American Tragedy—Detroit (1967), *126*

7. A Consensus of ~~

Figure 11. Urban Racial Violence in the Twentieth Century

that each chapter in Parts I and II groups specific riots by time period and classifies the riots by type, e.g. "The Effect of Job Competition." This book offers great possibilities for narrowing your topic by selecting one of these individual chapter headings. For example, you might choose to study the Watts Riot, one of the four protest riots mentioned in Chapter 6.

Possible Approaches to a Topic

It is easier to select and narrow a topic if you are aware of several possible approaches to a topic. This can be done even when the topic is arbitrarily assigned. Grant Morse, in his book, *Concise Guide to Library Research* (New York: Washington Square Press, 1967), pages 8 and 9, lists eight approaches to a topic. They are: bibliographical, biographical, chronological, geographical, linguistic, practical, statistical, or theoretical.

A *bibliographical* approach collects "resource materials in relation to a specific subject, author, or period. The list may be complete or selective. Brief descriptive or evaluative notes may be given with each work listed." For example, you could make a list of the best books and periodical articles on the Watts Riot and add evaluative annotations.

A *biographical* approach provides "factual information about the history of a person's life. This approach does not usually present all aspects of an individual's life." Example: The public career of Stokeley Carmichael.

The *chronological* approach gives an account of events in order of occurrence and may cover current or historical information. Example: The highlights of the Watts Riot.

A *geographical* approach "limits the topic to a given area." Example: A study of the social conditions in the Watts area of Los Angeles prior to the riot.

A *linguistic* approach is the study of language, its origin and development. Example: Trace the origin and meanings of the concept of racism.

A *practical* approach describes an "application of knowledge to some useful end. Such an approach is designed to supplement the purely theoretical view." Example: Preventing another Watts riot through the study of its causes.

A *theoretical* approach "deals with inferences drawn from the observed facts and the results of experiments." Example: Probable effects of racial riots in the 1960s on race relations in the 1970s.

A *statistical* approach collects, analyzes, interprets and presents numerical data. Example: Compilation of data on the damage caused by the Watts riot.

To illustrate how a broad topic could be narrowed by using a variety of reference sources, we selected "race relations in the United States" as an example. We suggested that the topic could be limited to racial riots occurring in the 1960s. This being still too large a topic, a further narrowing was made. Then we focused on one particular racial riot, the Los Angeles Watts riot. After further consultation of sources one aspect of the Los Angeles Watts riot, namely the "causes," was suggested. We could reduce the topic even further by focusing on one specific cause of the Watts riot.

I. Race Relations in the United States
   A. Racial Riots in the 1960s
      1. Los Angeles Watts riot
         a. Causes of the Riot
            1. One cause of the riot

Summary

1. It is vital to avoid writing on a topic that isn't too broad, because (a) you do not have time to write a book, (b) you do not have time to do extensive preparatory reading, and (c) you do not want to be superficial in covering a topic.

2. Narrow your topic as originally conceived by using any of the following: encyclopedias, textbooks, and reserve books; bibliographies, especially those arranged by subject; subject subdivisions in the card catalog; and tables of contents and indexes of books.

3. A topic can be narrowed through the following eight approaches to the subject: (1) bibliographical; (2) biographical; (3) chronological; (4) geographical; (5) linguistic; (6) practical; (7) theoretical; and (8) statistical.

The most immutable barrier in nature is between one man's thoughts and anothers.
William James

A library catalog is an index to the books in the library, just as the index of a book is the key to the contents of that particular book. The catalog also tells the following about each book: publisher, place, date, pages, height, subject matter, special features, and location in the library.

Book Catalogs and Card Catalogs

A library catalog can take various forms. Some library catalogs are in the form of printed books. Catalogs of this type have always been in use to some extent, and at one time they were the generally accepted form. However, book catalogs have largely been discarded as libraries grew in size, because cards for new materials could not be interfiled alphabetically. With the advent of photocopying devices, key-punch machines, and other inventions, the book catalog has come into use again. In computer-produced catalogs the entries may have full information or only two lines. It just depends on how much information was fed into the computer. The computer not only can make multiple copies of a catalog, but can interfile new entries in the old alphabet with each printing. Also, the information can be photographed on microfiche, a 3 by 5 inch card of microfilm which is used with a viewer.

Two advantages are claimed for the book catalog. First, it is easier to use; a larger number of entries can be seen at a glance since all books by an author follow each other on one or more pages. Second, duplicate copies of the catalog can be put several places on campus. The main disadvantages are that book catalogs are difficult to keep up to date, and it is time consuming to consult supplementary volumes.

Most library card catalogs are on 3 by 5 inch cards, and filed alphabetically in trays. There are many cross reference cards that refer from a heading that is not used to one that is or to additional headings.

Card catalogs are organized in several ways. Under one arrangement the author, subject, and title cards are divided into three alphabets. Or all three kinds of cards may be in one alphabet. Still another possibility is to have subject cards in one file, with author and title cards in another.

Limitations of the Catalog

In whatever form the library catalog appears, it is one of the most important sources that you can use in the library because, as stated earlier, it is an index to the book collection. But are you aware that the card catalog has some limitations? Do you know that it indexes only the *general* subjects of *books?* It does not usually index parts of books, nor does it provide access to periodical literature or government documents. Neither does it evaluate the books it lists. Also, did you know that the card catalog can be one of the hardest sources to use effectively?

The Language of Subject Headings

Of course, a catalog is usually simple to use if you need only a particular book and know its author and title. Then you just look up the book and copy its call number. The difficulty comes when you try to find what books the library has on a particular subject. Then you must cope with the special language of subject headings, which is so unlike spoken English that it could almost be considered a foreign language! Subject headings are arbitrary and knowing the correct subject heading is essential. Thus if you are to get the right response from the card catalog you must communicate with it in its own vocabulary. For example, the phrase "Racial Violence in the United States" would probably be in subject heading language "U.S. -- Race Question," or "Riots -- U.S." or "Race Problems." There is a dictionary to help you with the language of subject headings. It is *Library of Congress Subject Headings*, 9th ed., 2 vols. (Washington, DC: Library of Congress, 1980). This work and its supplements are a complete guide to the subject headings and cross references used in the card catalog. All headings are arranged alphabetically, including the cross references, that is, the "see" and "see also" references. These cross references are essential because subject headings, besides being arbitrarily chosen, are extremely numerous and occasionally changed. Some libraries expect readers to use *Library of Congress Subject Headings* and do not put "see" and "see also" cards in their catalogs. Those which do generally make only a minimal attempt to keep up with the large number of additions and changes in subject headings. Therefore you still need *Library of Congress Subject Headings*. However, you may have trouble finding it. Some libraries do not put it out, because it is prepared primarily for catalogers and is hard for the average student to use without help. You may need to ask your reference librarian to get this work for you and show you how to use it. If it is available, but without any sign or person to teach you to use it, study FIGURE 12 which will help you understand its use.

To summarize, "*sa*" and "*xx*" references are authorized for use in the card catalog; "*x*" references are not.

Besides using the subject heading book, you can also find subject headings printed at the bottom of catalog cards. These headings, called tracings, suggest related headings which you might otherwise miss. Sometimes the subject headings on catalog cards describe the content of a book more fully than does the title or subtitle. In FIGURE 13, the title of the book is *Social Control of Escalated Riots.* That by itself does not tell you that the book contains material on public relations concerning police. But the last subject heading brings out this topic. The second subject heading "U.S. -- Race question," tells you that racial riots are being discussed.

A basic rule in using subject headings is to look first under the one that most precisely describes your topic; then,

if you need more books, turn to broader or related headings. For example, as FIGURE 12 shows, the most precise headings for your topic, racial violence in the United States, are "Riots," as well as the subject subdivision "riots" under the names of cities, e.g. "Detroit -- Riots," and specific riot names, e.g., "Los Angeles, Watts Riot, 1965." Broader and related subject headings might be "Riots," "Street fighting (Military Science)," "Mobs," and "Breach of the Peace."

After having read carefully the suggestions on the interpretation and use of the card catalog, do you now feel at least a little more confident about finding the right subject headings? Finding the right subject headings is so important and so difficult, (even with the *Library of Congress Subject Headings*), that it is never safe to assume that you have found everything about your topic that might be found in the card catalog. Asking for help at the Reference Desk is generally advisable when you are trying to cope with subject headings. The right subject headings can so easily elude

---

1. **Subject headings in bold print are authorized for use. "Riots" is such a heading.**

2. **Dashes indicate subject subdivisions. "Riots -- Research" is such a subdivision.**

3. **"*sa*" stands for "*see also*" and refers to one or more related subject headings. One of the nine "*sa*" or related subject headings under "Riots" is "Mobs."**

4. **"*xx*" has almost the same meaning as "*sa*" directly above, and refers to one or more related subject headings.**

5. **"*See*" references refer from headings which are not used to those which are.**

6. **"*x*" preceeds headings which are *not* found in the catalog and refers you to the correct headings that are in bold print above.**

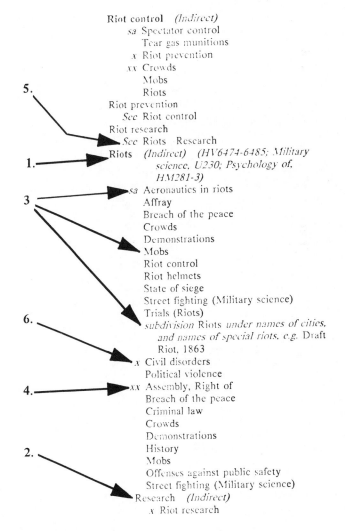

Figure 12. **Library of Congress Subject Headings**

```
                RIOTS--U.S.
    HV      Janowitz, Morris
    6477        Social control of escalated riots.   [Chicago]
    J8      University of Chicago, Center for Policy Study
            [1968]
                44 p.   26 cm.

            "Prepared for the Center's conference on 'Short
            Term Measure to Avert Urban Violence.'"
            Bibliographical footnotes.


                1. Riots--U.S.   2. U.S.--Race question.   3.
            Public relations--Police.   I. Chicago.  University
            Center for Policy Study.   II. Title.
```

Figure 13. Catalog card

you, and when they do, important books will also elude you.

If you don't find the right subject heading you may also miss periodical articles and other materials because the same subject headings used in the card catalog are widely used in other reference sources. Use of the card catalog is part of your reference librarian's area of expertise, since she or he communicates with it all day long. Do not hesitate to consult with a librarian. Librarians are there to help you.

Summary

1. A library's catalog may be a card catalog or a catalog in book form.
2. A library catalog is limited because it indexes only the *general* subjects of books, and it does not evaluate them.
3. The language of subject headings is complex and arbitrary. The best guide to subject headings is *Library of Congress Subject Headings*. Subject headings preceded by "*sa*" and "*xx*" are authorized for use in the card catalog, but headings preceded by "x" are not.
4. Look first under the subject headings that most precisely describe your topic. Then use broader or related headings.

The best things and best people rise out of their separateness; I'm against a homogenized society because I want the cream to rise.
Robert Frost

Browsing

A chapter, or even a part of a chapter, may be all you need from a book, and yet it can be vital for your term paper. How do you find the parts that you need? In this guide you have already learned that the card catalog does not index parts of books. However, by looking in the tables of contents and indexes of books on the shelves in appropriate subject areas of the stacks, you can often discover chapters that could be useful.

Browsing works because library books are classified by subject in order to bring together on a shelf books that deal with the same topic. Similar books in the Dewey Decimal Classification will have the same numbers on the top line of the call number; in the Library of Congress Classification similar books will have the same top two and sometimes three lines.

To be an effective browser, begin with a cluster of the most precise subject headings on your topic and note the call numbers of the most promising books found under these

Contents

PREFACE	xi
1: Violence as Protest	1
2: Who Riots?	27
3: From Resentment to Confrontation	53
4: The Ghetto's Grievances	79
5: The Erosion of Restraint	105
6: The Moderates' Dilemma	129
7: Liberalism at an Impasse	155
EPILOGUE	183
APPENDIX: White on Black	191
NOTES	217
INDEX	255

Looting, 17, 45–46, 50, 79 ff., 86–90, 99, 102 (*See also* specific places); survey on shooting of looters, 179
Los Angeles, California, xiv, 3, 4, 10, 14, 17, 24 ff., 27, 30, 53, 54, 77, 79, 91, 97–98, 107, 112–19 *passim*, 129, 139, 185, 186, 189, 191–216 (*See also* McCone Commission); buying of weapons by whites, 188; and civilian complaints on police, 71; election of conservative mayor, 180; Mexicans and Japanese, 99; and police brutality, harassment, 58, 62–63, 64, 66, 71, 200 ff., 211; and pride of place, 140; probability of substantial minority of blacks, 150; schools, 88; slogan of riots, 15; statistics on crime, 67; statistics on rioters, 31 ff., 41, 49, 50, 113, 195 ff.; and territoriality in Watts, 96; World War II riots, 6
Los Angeles County Human Relations Commission, 191

Figure 14. From Violence As Protest by Robert M. Fogelson. Copyright © 1971 by Robert M. Fogelson. Used by permission of Doubleday & Company, Inc.

Riots

Clark, K. B. "The wonder is there have been so few riots"
   In Endleman, S. ed. Violence in the streets p287-95

Endleman, S. The etiology of the race riot
   In Endleman, S. ed. Violence in the streets p357-61

Hamilton, C. V. Riots, revolts and relevant response
   In Barbour, F. B. ed. The Black Power revolt p171-78

Leary, H. R. The role of the police in riotous demonstrations
   In Endleman, S. ed. Violence in the streets p369-80

United States. National Advisory Commission on Civil Disorders. Report of the National Advisory Commission on Civil Disorders—summary
   In Blaustein, A. I. and Woock, R. R. eds. Man against poverty: World War III p176-84

See also Subdivision Riots under names of cities, e.g. Los Angeles

Los Angeles

Race question

Pynchon, T. Journey into the mind of Watts
   In Blaustein, A. I. and Woock, R. R. eds. Man against poverty: World War III p146-58

Riots, 1965

California. Governor's Commission on the Los Angeles Riots. 144 hours in August 1965
   In Endleman, S. ed. Violence in the streets p319-32

Cohen, N. E. The Los Angeles riot study
   In Endleman, S. ed. Violence in the streets p333-46

Cooke, A. Topic A: 1965—Watts
   In Cooke, A. Talk about America p253-58

Howard, J. and McCord, W. Watts: the revolt and after
   In Life styles in the black ghetto p52-68

McCord, W. and Howard, J. Collective styles of life
   In Life styles in the black ghetto p258-95

Rustin, B. Some lessons from Watts
   In Endleman, S. ed. Violence in the streets p347-56

LIST OF BOOKS INDEXED

Endleman, Shalom
   (ed.) Violence in the streets; ed. with an introduction by Shalom Endleman. Quadrangle Bks. 1968
      Partially analyzed
Engaged & disengaged. See Bush, D.
Engler, Richard E.
   The challenge of diversity, by Richard E. Engler, Jr. Harper 1964

Figure 15. Essay and General Literature Index

headings. When you get to these books on the shelves, look not only at them but also at the other books with the same subject classification, as described in the previous paragraph. Be sure to examine the indexes in all these books, as well as their tables of contents.

As shown in FIGURE 14, the table of contents in Fogelson's *Violence as Protest* might cause you to wonder if any pages deal with the Los Angeles riot, because none of the chapter titles mention this subject. But when you look up "Los Angeles, California" in the index, also shown in FIGURE 17, you discover exactly which pages deal with your topic. The longest sections are pages 191--216 and 112--119.

Using the *Essay and General Literature Index*

Another way to locate appropriate parts of books is to use a reference source entitled *Essay and General Literature Index, 1900--1933*, edited by M.E. Sears and M. Shaw (New York: Wilson, 1934) and its *Supplements* (New York: Wilson, 1937--). This is a detailed index to essays and articles published in book form from 1900 to the present. It is excellent for locating narrow or unusual subjects not covered by whole books. It is also a good source to consult for biographical and critical material about persons, as well as criticisms of individual books. This index does not duplicate what you may find in subject bibliographies, because they rarely cite individual essays.

Use of this index requires three steps. First, to locate recent essays on riots, look under the correct subject headings, most of which are identical to those used in the card catalog. Notice the instruction in FIGURE 15 to look under names of cities with the sub-division "riots." Here you find a thirteen page article written by N.E. Cohen, entitled "The Los Angeles Riot Study," in a book edited by S. Endleman and entitled *Violence in the Streets*.

Second, look in the "List of Books Indexed" in the back of the volume, under whatever word follows "*In*" in the citation, e.g. "Endleman, S." in the above illustration. This gives the full bibliographic information on the book. Third, look up that book (Endleman's *Violence in the Streets*) in the card catalog to see if your library owns it.

Summary

1. A chapter or a few pages may be all you need from a book.
2. Browsing will uncover useful pages that cannot be found through the card catalog or through bibliographies.
3. The *Essay and General Literature Index* is used to locate essays and miscellaneous articles, most of which would otherwise have remained buried in the card catalog under broad subject headings.

One of your tasks as a term-paper writer will be to find the better books and avoid the worse. Books selected from the card catalog should be evaluated to determine if they are the best available on your topic. For example, if your paper stands or falls on the reliability of the facts and interpretations of Cohen's *The Los Angeles Riots: A Socio-Psychological Study* or Conot's *Rivers of Blood, Years of Darkness*, you will want to be certain that these books are trustworthy. You will want to know if other scholars supported, questioned, or rejected their ideas.

Selective Bibliographies

A book can probably be trusted if it appears on an authoritative, selective bibliography in the field. A good example is the one excerpted from *Blacks in America; Bibliographical Essays* and shown again in FIGURE 16. This bibliography has several characteristics which make it almost ideal for a student writing a paper on the causes of the Watts riot. First, it is authoritative, having been selected by a team of Princeton professors. Second, it is selective; its paragraph on riots in various cities lists only six of the most important books on Watts, whereas a really comprehensive bibliography would list many more. Third, it includes periodical articles. Fourth, it is arranged by subject, and the subject mentioned above is on our proposed topic. Fifth, it comments on the books so that you can know more about them than their titles. For example, it helps to know that the book edited by Bullock "affords an invaluable perspective on why and how Watts happened." Sixth, it is relatively up-to-date, having been published in 1971.

It is worth hunting for such a bibliography because it can save you time in your search and allow you to proceed more confidently. This bibliography provides some of the basic reading, but of course it would need to be supplemented by articles, book reviews, government documents, and other bibliographies found in all these sources.

Finding Book Reviews

Don't judge a book by its cover, and, as was stressed in Chapter 3, don't judge a book only from its catalog card either. This is why bibliographies and book reviews are so indispensable.

A book can probably be trusted if it appears on the selective, authoritative bibliographies in the field. However, when it comes to evaluating a book, book reviews are more helpful than selective bibliographies. Four useful sources for locating book reviews are: *Book Review Digest, Book Review Index, Current Book Review Citations*, and *Social Sciences Citation Index.*

Book Review Digest (New York: Wilson, 1905--) gives excerpts from book reviews in approximately seventy-five periodicals and tells where the complete review is published. Most are general in nature, but fifteen major social science journals are included. The entries are arranged by author with subject and title indexes. To use *Book Review Digest*, look in the volume which corresponds to the earliest publication date of the book, as well as the year following. If the book does not appear in either of those volumes, you will not find it in *Book Review Digest*. Such reviews need to be found by other strategies.

To find a review of Nathan Cohen's *The Los Angeles Riots: A Socio-Psychological Study*, published in 1971, start with the 1971 volume of Book Review Digest. FIGURE 17 shows that under Cohen you will find an excerpt of a review of his book from the *American Journal of Sociology*, reference to a review in the *American Sociological Review*, and also a publisher's note. You can decode "Am J Soc" by looking on a front page of the *Book Review Digest* where abbreviations are spelled out. "76:770 Ja '71 600w" means volume 76, page 770, January, 1971, and the complete review is about 600 words long. To read the full text of the reviews from the sociology journals, go to the periodical shelves. According to this excerpt from a 1971 review, Cohen's book "is undoubtedly the most important study of an interracial disturbance now available."

Book Review Index (Detroit: Gale Research, 1965--) indexes reviews in over 200 periodicals, which is about three times more than are covered by *Book Review Digest*. *Book Review Index* covers eleven sociology journals whereas *Book Review Digest* currently covers only one, the *American Journal of Sociology*. Reviews in scholarly journals often appear more than two years after a book is published, so they would not be reported by *Book Review Digest* but would appear in *Book Review Index*. The only two disadvantages of *Book Review Index*, in comparison with *Book Review Digest*, are that it provides no excerpts; and it cites no reviews before 1965. Take a look at FIGURE 18 which shows that *Book Review Index* cites twelve reviews of Robert Conot's *Rivers of Blood, Years of Darkness*. *Book Review Digest* cites only five reviews of this book.

There is already a voluminous literature analyzing the riot phenomenon and chronicling outbreaks in various cities. Harlem is treated in Fred C. Shapiro and James W. Sullivan, *Race Riots: New York, 1964* (New York, 1964). Lenora E. Berson, *Case Study of a Riot: The Philadelphia Story* (New York, 1966), is a pamphlet on the 1964 outbreak in that city. Among the individual riots, Watts has received the most intensive coverage to date. Robert E. Conot gives what is probably the best narrative account of Watts by an outsider in *Rivers of Blood, Years of Darkness* (Toronto, Ont., 1967),* but Jerry Cohen and William S. Murphy, *Burn, Baby, Burn! The Los Angeles Race Riot, August, 1965* (New York, 1966), and Spencer Crump, *Black Riot in Los Angeles: The Story of the Watts Tragedy* (Los Angeles, 1966), should also be consulted. Paul Bullock, ed., ***Watts: The Aftermath; An Inside View of the Ghetto by the People of Watts*** (New York, 1970),* affords an invaluable perspective on why and how Watts happened. Nathan Cohen, ed., *The Los Angeles Riots: A Socio-Psychological Study* (New York, 1970), is extremely thorough and informative. See also David O. Sears and T. M. Tomlinson, "Riot Ideology in Los Angeles: A Study of Negro Attitudes," *SSQ*, XLIX (Dec. 1968), 485–503, which also appears as ch. 30 of Glenn and Bonjean, eds., *Blacks in the United States*, cited above; Anthony Oberschall, "The Los Angeles Riot of August 1965," *Social Problems*, XV (Winter 1968), 322–41; H. Edward Ransford, "Isolation, Powerlessness, and Violence: A Study of Attitudes and Participation in the Watts Riot," *AJS*, LXXIII (Mar. 1968), 581–91;** and "Watts, 1965," in Richard Hofstadter and Michael Wallace, eds., *American Violence: A Documentary History* (New York, 1970),* pp. 263–66. The official report of the Governor's Commission on the Los Angeles Riots (the McCone Commission), *Violence in the City—An End or a Beginning?* (Los Angeles, 1965), has been the subject of much criticism; for a sample of views, see Paul Jacobs, *Prelude to Riot: A View of Urban America from the Bottom* (New York, 1967),* a detailed analysis of black grievances in Los Angeles; Robert M. Fogelson, "White on Black: A Critique of the McCone Commission Report on the Los Angeles Riots," *PSQ*, LXXXII (Sept. 1967), 337–67;** Bayard Rustin, "The Watts 'Manifesto' and the McCone Report," *Commentary*, XLI (Mar. 1966), 29–35; and Robert Blauner, "Whitewash over Watts," *Trans-action*, III (Mar.–Apr. 1966), 9.

COHEN, NATHAN, ed. The Los Angeles riots;
a socio-psychological study; pub. in coop.
with the Inst. of gov. and public affairs,
Univ. of Calif, Los Angeles. 742p $20 Praeger
309.1794 Los Angeles—Riots. Negroes—Los
Angeles
LC 73-94248

This "study of the 1965 Watts riots contains
. . . . data on pre-riot social and political conditions in Los Angeles, the effects of the riots
on Negro-white racial attitudes, police actions
before and after the riots, and reforms since
that . . . summer. Researchers . . . [list] the
basic causes of discontent among Negroes. . . .
The study participants conclude that there has
been only a negligible response to Negro needs
since the riots." (Publisher's note) Index.

"An interdisciplinary team from the UCLA
faculty [produced this study]. . . . The
principal empirical endeavors were a field
survey of 585 blacks in the curfew area
and a field survey of 583 whites from selected neighborhoods. The questions asked
were of immediate public or practical interest,
but they are formulated and the data analyzed
with sufficient sophistication to be amenable
to serious theoretical interpretation. . . . In
spite of any limitations, the range of questions
investigated, the sophistication with which
questions were designed to answer these questions, and the high standards of data collection and analysis make this undoubtedly the
most important study of an interracial disturbance now available. It is unfortunate that
work of this importance should have been
published in typescript-offset and priced at
the discouraging figure of $20.00." R. H. Tur-
ner
Am J Soc 76:770 Ja '71 600w
Reviewed by R. H. Friis
Am Soc R 36:943 O '71 700w

Figure 17. Book Review Digest

Still broader coverage of reviews in periodicals is provided by *Current Book Review Citations* (New York: Wilson,
1976--) and by *Social Sciences Citation Index* (Philadelphia:
Institute for Scientific Information, 1972--). *Current Book
Review Citations* is issued monthly with annual cumulations
and indexes all the reviews in all the periodical indexes published by the H.W. Wilson Company. Since Wilson publishes
not only the *Readers' Guide, Social Sciences Index*, and
Humanities Index, but also periodical indexes for art, business, education, law, and library science, this is a tremendous
resource. It covers more than 1,000 periodicals having book
reviews. Almost all libraries have *Current Book Review Citations*, and it is easy to use because it is so like the *Readers'
Guide*. Book reviews are cited under the author's name, but
if you know only the title you can use its title index to find
the author. Too bad it didn't begin until 1976.

Social Sciences Citation Index covers some 1,000 social
sciences periodicals, a good many more than are covered
by *Current Book Review Citations*, which includes many
general interest and humanities periodicals among its more
than 1,000 titles. Probably its major limitation is that not
too many libraries own it because it is so expensive.

If no reviews are found in the above sources, or if more
are needed, there are other possibilities. Periodical indexes
for other disciplines can be used when they correspond to
the subject matter of your book. Some examples are: *Education Index, Index to Legal Periodicals*, and *Religion Index
One: Periodicals*. Book reviews may be cited in various

parts of a periodical index. Sometimes they are in a separate section in the book; sometimes they are in the main
alphabet under the subject heading "Book reviews."

Another possibility for finding reviews is to search
through individual periodicals which do not have their reviews cited by a periodical index. As you have seen, the
older the date of publication, the fewer indexes to book reviews are available. Of course, searching individual periodicals
is very time consuming. There is no way to know whether a
review will appear during the year of publication or three
years later. Also, not all books published are reviewed. Some
periodicals make the chore a little faster because they publish their own indexes which you will find in the front or
back of each bound volume. Book reviews may be indexed
here under the headings of "book reviews," "reviews," or
"criticism." They may also appear in a separate section.
Your reference librarian may have a subject list of your library's periodicals, so that you can choose which periodicals
to search.

Biographical Information to Judge an Author's Competence

All is not lost if you cannot find a review of a book that
is central to your paper. You can often get a good idea about
an author's competence and social background by finding a
review of another book by the same author. Another strategy
is to find biographical information that indicates whether
the author of your book is considered an authority in his
field. His occupation, education, and publications are all
ways to measure his authority and social background.

In considering an author's occupation, notice his field
of endeavor (whether it is sociology or another field), along
with the status of his place of employment, and his rank.
(The pecking order in higher education is: professor, associ-

CONNOR, William - Cassandra
Manch Guard - D. Barker - v 97 - 2 Nov 67 - p 10
CONOT, Robert - Rivers of Blood, Years of Darkness
Bk World - G. Levitas - v 1 - 17 Sep 67 - p 15
Bks Today - C. Petersen - v 4 - 2 Jul 67 - p 8
Dissent - L. Coser - v 14 - Sep/Oct 67 - p 611
Lib Jnl - C. M. Weisenberg - v 92 - 1 Sep 67 - p 2938
Nation - L. Kampf - v 205 - 14 Aug 67 - p 117
Natl Observer - D. M. Davis - v 6 - 31 Jul 67 - p 17
N Y Times (D) - R. Jellinek - v 116 - 4 Aug 67 - p 31M
N Y Times Bk Rev - R. M. Elman - v 72 - 20 Aug 67 - p 3
Pub Wkly - v 191 - 19 Jun 67 - p 85
Sat Rev - H. R. Mayes - v 50 - 1 Jul 67 - p 6
Sat Rev - E. M. Yoder, Jr. - v 50 - 26 Aug 67 - p 28
Time - v 90 - 11 Aug 67 - p 74
CONOVER, David B. - Once Upon an Island
Kirkus - v 35 - 15 Sep 67 - p 1169
Pub Wkly - v 192 - 25 Sep 67 - p 98

Figure 18. Book Review Index

ate professor, assistant professor, and instructor.) To illustrate all these variables at once, a book on racial riots is probably more reliable if it is written by a full professor of sociology at Harvard University than if it is written by an instructor of speech at a junior college. However, this way of evaluating a person is sometimes dead wrong. A book by an instructor could be better than a book by a full professor.

Sources of Biographical Information

Some writers you may recognize at once as being authorities either because your professor may have put one or more of their books or articles on reserve or because you remember their names from one of the selective bibliographies. Others you may not recognize at all. In looking for biographical information you can save time selecting biographical sources if you know whether your person is living or dead, along with her or his occupation and nationality.

Since you are doing a paper for a sociology class, you will want to read respected sociologists. Also, since your topic is "racial riots" and specifically the causes of the 1965 Watts Riot in Los Angeles, you will want contemporary reports written by living sociologists, both black and white. Therefore you will select biographical sources listing living persons as opposed to those listing deceased persons. Since your topic is an American problem you will consult directories listing Americans. Two excellent biographical sources on contemporary American sociologists are: the Social and Behavioral Sciences volumes of *American Men and Women of Science*, 12th ed., 8 vols. (New York: Jaques Cattell/ Bowker, 1973) and the American Sociological Association *Directory* (New York, 1950–). The American Sociological Association publishes a triennial directory of its members which includes persons from other nations as well as the United States. This directory is arranged alphabetically by name, then has a geographical listing, and finally, as shown in FIGURE 19, a listing by subject competency. Information that is included is: name, birth date, education, employment, area of sociological competence, and major publications. For example, FIGURE 19 shows that Seymour Spilerman was born in 1938, received a Ph.D. in sociology from Johns Hopkins University in 1968, is currently a full professor at the University of Wisconsin, specializes in race/ethnic/ minority relations and mathematical sociology. The 12th edition of *American Men and Women of Science* has six volumes for the physical and biological scientists and two volumes for the social and behavioral sciences. These two volumes include persons active in the fields of psychology, sociology, geography, anthropology, economics, political science, and statistics. Biographical information that is included is: birth date, education and training, employment and major publications.

A handy way to find biographical information on living as well as deceased sociologists, as well as other professionals, is by using *Biography Index*, 1946– (New York: Wilson, 1947–). This indexes biographical material that appears in

Spiggle, Susan (SM) 1945, f; Instr; Dept of Soc, U of Hartford, West Hartford, CT 06117; BA 68, Coll of Wm & Mary; MA 70, U of Connecticut, soc; marriage & family, strat/mobility; 161 Cameo Gardens, Willimantic, CT 06226.

Spilerman, Seymour (MB) 1938, m; Prof; Dept of Soc, U of Wisconsin, Madison, WI 53706; BA 59, Pomona Coll; MA 61, Brandeis U; PhD 68, Johns Hopkins U, soc; race/ethnic/minority rel, mathematical soc; 3106 Bluff, Madison, WI 53705.

Spiller, Bertram (MB) 1919, m; Assoc Prof; Chair; Dept of Soc, U of Bridgeport, Bridgeport, CT 06602; BS 42, Northeastern U; MA 48, PhD 61, Boston U, soc; criminology/delinquency, deviant bhvr/social disorg; 1124 North Benson Rd, Fairfield, CT 06430.

RACE/ETHNIC/MINORITY RELATIONS

Snyder, Kay Ann
Somers, Eldon K
Sparks, Lois R
Spiegel, John P
Spilerman, Seymour
Spruell, Malcolm E
St John, Nancy H
Stabler, George M
Stack, Norman A

Figure 19. American Sociological Association, 1975/1976, Directory of Members

periodical articles, books, and chapters in books of collective biography. The format of this source is the same as the *Readers' Guide to Periodical Literature*. The main section consists of entries arranged alphabetically by the name of the person. As an example, FIGURE 20 cites a book and an article about Emiles Durkheim, the distinguished sociologist. This is followed by a listing of the biographies organized by profession or occupation. As FIGURE 20 shows, sociologists are included in the index to professions or occupations. All

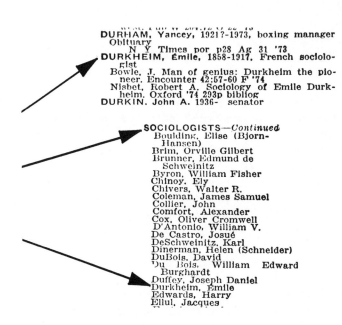

DURHAM, Yancey, 1921?-1973, boxing manager
Obituary
N Y Times por p28 Ag 31 '73
DURKHEIM, Émile, 1858-1917, French sociologist
Bowle, J. Man of genius: Durkheim the pioneer. Encounter 42:57-60 F '74
Nisbet, Robert A. Sociology of Emile Durkheim. Oxford '74 293p bibliog
DURKIN, John A. 1936- senator

SOCIOLOGISTS—*Continued*
Boulding, Elise (Bjorn-Hansen)
Brim, Orville Gilbert
Brunner, Edmund de Schweinitz
Byron, William Fisher
Chinoy, Ely
Chivers, Walter R.
Coleman, James Samuel
Collier, John
Comfort, Alexander
Cox, Oliver Cromwell
D'Antonio, William V.
De Castro, Josué
DeSchweinitz, Karl
Dinerman, Helen (Schneider)
DuBois, David
Du Bois, William Edward Burghardt
Duffey, Joseph Daniel
Durkheim, Émile
Edwards, Harry
Ellul, Jacques

Figure 20. Biography Index

biographies are American unless otherwise indicated.

There are several other biographical sources that cover contemporaries in all fields. *Contemporary Authors* (Detroit: Gale, 1962–) gives biographical and bibliographical data on some fifty thousand writers. *Who's Who in America* (Chicago: Marquis-Who's Who, 1899–), is a biennial that presents in condensed form the basic data on about sixty thousand living American V.I.P.s. *Who's Who* (New York: St. Martin's Press, 1849–) is published annually and carries data on important living Britons. *International Who's Who* (London: Europa, 1935–) and *Who's Who in the World* (Chicago: Marquis, 1970–) can help you find out about sociologists living in other countries.

Perhaps your author is no longer living. In that case try the *New York Times Obituary Index, 1858--1968* (New York: New York Times, 1970) or *Who Was Who in America, 1607--* (Chicago: Marquis, 1942–) or, for Britons, *Who Was Who, 1897--* (London: Black, 1935–).

The biographical sources listed in this chapter are some of the basic ones that will help you get started in your biographical searches. Knowing the persons' field of endeavor, whether they are alive or dead, and what nationality they are, will determine what biographical sources to consult.

Summary

1. Try to select the best books on your topic and avoid the worse.
2. *Book Review Digest* provides excerpts from book reviews in about seventy-five periodicals beginning 1905.
3. *Book Review Index* began in 1965 and covers about 200 periodicals.
4. *Current Book Review Citations* began in 1976 and covers more than 1,000 periodicals.
5. *Social Sciences Citation Index* indexes reviews in some 1,000 social sciences periodicals beginning 1972.
6. Periodical indexes for other disciplines contain book reviews in education.
7. As a last resort, look in individual periodicals not covered by a periodical index. Many have an index in each bound volume.
8. If you can't find a book review, look for biographical information in order to judge an author's competence.
9. American Sociological Association *Directory, Who's Who in America*, and other Who's Who-type sources provide brief biographical sketches.
10. *Biography Index* is an index to books and articles about people.
11. Deceased people can be located through the *New York Times Obituary Index* and several other sources.

Happy the man, and happy he alone, He who can call today his own.
John Dryden, *Imitations of Horace*.

Why Periodical Articles Are Important

Periodical articles, newspapers, and pamphlets are indispensable for the study of currently debated topics. The latest word cannot be found in books, because of the length of time it takes for one to be published. The manuscript of a book may be two or more years older than its publication date, whereas the time elapsed between the writing of an article in a periodical or pamphlet and the date of its publication is not nearly as great. For rapidly changing issues, the latest information and insights are needed and these can only be supplied by periodicals, newspapers, and pamphlets.

Periodicals can also be invaluable as supplements to books. In this case you need not depend on the latest periodicals. Earlier ones may do just as well. For example, if books fail to give you enough discussion of the various causes of racial violence, you might benefit from looking at scholarly periodical articles. Locating such articles is not a hopeless task, thanks to all the people who have put together various periodical indexes. You are probably familiar with the *Readers' Guide to Periodical Literature*, which indexes such popular periodicals as *Time, Newsweek*, and *Reader's Digest*. However, you may not be familiar with some other, more specialized, indexes which can be found in most libraries and are much more helpful for covering the literature of sociology.

First Use the *Social Sciences Index*

The *Social Sciences Index* (New York: Wilson, 1974–) is the first periodical index for sociology students to use because it covers more than twenty of the most important scholarly journals in sociology. These are the sociology journals most likely to be in a college library. From 1965 to 1974 this index was entitled *Social Sciences & Humanities Index* and from 1907 to 1965 it was entitled *International Index*. The *Social Sciences Index* is easy to use because its format is identical to that of the *Readers' Guide to Periodical Literature*. (When using the *Readers' Guide* be sure to select articles written by reputable scholars, who often write for such semi-scholarly periodicals as *Saturday Review* and *Atlantic*.)

In FIGURE 21, taken from the *Social Sciences & Humanities Index*, note that by looking under "Los Angeles" you can find four references to the Watts riot of 1965, three of them from sociology journals. Along with its subject

approach this index also has a listing under the authors' names.

Next Use *Sociological Abstracts*

The next place for sociology students to seek recent periodical articles is *Sociological Abstracts* (New York, 1953–), which currently comes out five times a year and annually publishes abstracts, i.e. summaries, of approximately 250 books and over 5,000 articles appearing in over 200 journals, including thirty-one major sociological journals. Journals in related fields are partially abstracted for articles related to sociology. *Sociological Abstracts* should be used to supplement *Social Sciences Index*. If you do not find what you need in the latter, go to the former. Also, if *Social Sciences Index* cites an article not in your library that you think you may want to get hold of, then look up its abstract in *Sociological Abstracts*. The abstract will probably make it easy to decide whether you need to request a photocopy from another library. More on this later.

The best way to approach a topic is by looking in the index of the most recent volumes. Under the subject heading "riots– –ing" in the example shown in FIGURE 22, there

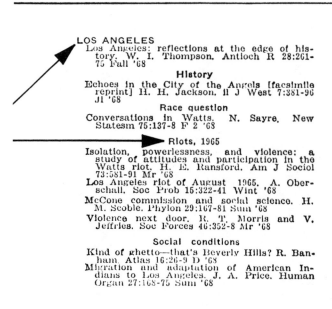

Figure 21. Social Sciences & Humanities Index

are several references to the Los Angeles Watts riot: 10 F3496, 27 F3691, and 28 F3721. The first two numbers can be ignored because they refer to the major subject sections within each issue, e.g., "10" refers to "social differentiation." Note the last five letters and numbers of the abstracts and look them up in the main section of the issue. FIGURE 22 shows abstract F3474, which comes between abstracts F3473 and F3475.

Three Other Sources for Recent Articles

Perhaps the next place to look for recent articles is *Public Affairs Information Service Bulletin* (New York: Public Affairs Information Service, 1915–), often called *PAIS*. This is a selective subject list of the latest books, pamphlets, government publications, reports of public and private agencies and periodical articles, relating to economic and social conditions, public administration, and international relations which are published in English throughout the world. It can be especially useful to you because it indexes some sociology journals, such as the *Journal of Current Social Issues*, that are not in the *Social Sciences Index*. However, its coverage is very selective. If a periodical ap-

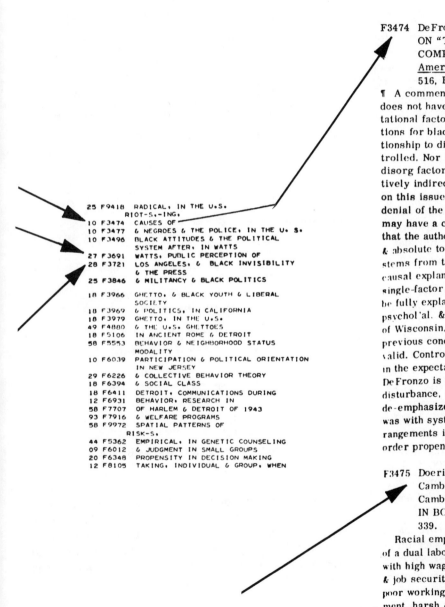

F3474 De Fronzo, James (Indiana U, Fort Wayne), COMMENT ON "THE CAUSES OF RACIAL DISTURBANCES:" A COMPARISON OF ALTERNATIVE EXPLANATIONS, American Sociological Review, 1971, 36, 3, Jun 515-516, REPLY, 516-517.

¶ A comment on SA 0410/E7022. It is noted that Spilerman does not have empirical justification for rejecting the "expectational factors" (both absolutely & relatively better life conditions for blacks in disorder-prone cities) because their relationship to disorders disappears when size of black pop is controlled. Nor is Spilerman's rejection of the importance of soc disorg factors warranted, since his measures of it are relatively indirect, & he fails to adequately consider previous res on this issue. Disagreement is also voiced with Spilerman's denial of the possibility that unresponsive pol'al structures may have a causal signif for riots. Spilerman's study suffers that the author has made conclusions which are far too general & absolute to be justified by his methods. Part of the problem stems from the way in which r'al data were used to arrive at a causal explanation for disorders which resulted in a narrow single-factor explanation for a soc phenomenon which can only be fully explained through a combination of demographic, soc psychol'al. & soc structural variables. Seymour Spilerman (U of Wisconsin, Madison), REPLY TO De FRONZO—reaffirms his previous conclusions, pointing out why they must be considered valid. Controlling Negro pop size did not reduce the variation in the expectational indicators by any substantial extent. If De Fronzo is arguing that there are idiosyncratic causes of a disturbance, then Spilerman agrees. But Spilerman wished to de-emphasize these particularistic factors, since his concern was with systematic causes: whether certain structural arrangements in a community characteristically make for disorder propensity. M. Maxfield

F3475 Doeringer, Peter B. & Michael J. Plore (Harvard U, Cambridge, Mass & Massachusetts Instit of Technology, Cambridge), EQUAL EMPLOYMENT OPPORTUNITY IN BOSTON, Industrial Relations, 1970, 9, 3, May, 324-339.

Racial employment practices in Boston are analyzed in terms of a dual labor market: (a) the primary sector, offering jobs with high wages, good working conditions, employment stabil'' & job security; (b) the secondary sector, involv'' poor working conditions, considerab' ment, harsh & often arb'' to advance

Figure 22. Sociological Abstracts

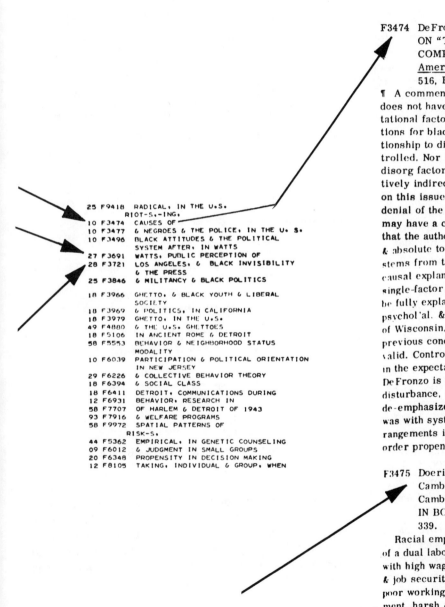

pears in the list in front, it means that at least one reference to it is made in the volume. In this it differs from most periodical indexes, which index every article of the journals they include. *PAIS* selectively covers more periodicals than any of the other indexes described in this chapter, except for *Social Sciences Citation Index*.

A specialized periodical index that is useful for this term-paper topic is the *Index to Periodical Articles by and about Blacks* (Boston: Hall, 1950–). This covers fifty-six periodicals from the Hallie Q. Brown Memorial Library at Central State University in Wilberforce, Ohio. It provides easy access to Black points of view, which should not be overlooked in a term paper on racial riots. As FIGURE 23 shows, articles under the subject heading "riots" are arranged under the names of various cities.

Human Resources Abstracts (Beverly Hills, CA: Sage, 1966–) is another specialized abstracting service useful for this topic. It puts emphasis on "research and action" programs and legislative and community developments, as well as policy trends in the social problems area. It includes abstracts of periodical articles, books, pamphlets, and unpublished reports that are mainly concerned with the United States.

A Time-saver

C.R.I.S.; The Combined Retrospective Index Set to Journals in Sociology, 1895--1974, 6 vols. (Washington, DC: Carrollton, 1978) is a monumental work that provides an author and subject index to 129 English language sociology periodicals. Some 105,000 articles are arranged in the five subject volumes under eighty-six broad categories, which are further subdivided by key words taken from the titles of articles.

When you look in the section headed "Group Interactions; Race & Ethnic Relations," as shown in FIGURE 24, you find several articles on the Los Angeles Watts riots cited under "riot," "rioters," "riots," and "Watts" as key words. One of the "reference titles" (not necessarily the title of the article) is "Negro & Church Following Los Angeles Riot," which is by J.B. McConahay, published in 1970, in volume 31, starting on page 12 of journal number 800. To find out the title of journal number 800, look inside the back cover. As shown, number 800 is *Sociological Analysis*, a journal that is not covered by *Social Sciences Index*.

Because *C.R.I.S.; The Combined Retrospective Index Set to Journals in Sociology, 1895--1974* gives such quick access to so many journals, it is a great time saver. You can manage pretty well by using it in conjunction with other indexes covering 1975 to date. The unpleasant alternative is to dig through many volumes of several periodical indexes, such as the *International Index*, and even then you will not cover as many titles as are in C.R.I.S. However, *C.R.I.S.* has several weaknesses. Some of its key word subject headings do not work effectively. For example, "Negro" gives you five

RIOTS

A call for national action, statement of The Emergency Convocation of The Urban Coalition. New South 22:77-80 Fall '67

Historical roots of the riots. Freedomways 7:60-63 Winter '67

Race riots, Harlem and Bedford-Stuyvesant: an editorial. Interracial Rev 37:138-140 Jl '64

Revolt in the ghettos; an essay-review of five books and pamphlets on race riots, historical and recent, in various cities in the United States. Freedomways 7:34-41 Winter '67

The Springfield race riot of 1908. J of Negro Hist pp164-181 Jl '60

Atlanta, Georgia

Racial violence and social reform. Origins of the Atlanta riot of 1906. J of Negro Hist 53:234-256 Jl '68

Atlanta, Georgia riot of 1906

Racial massacre in Atlanta Sept. 22, 1906. J of Negro Hist. 54:150-173 Ap '69

Chicago, Illinois

The day the "race war" struck Chicago, July 27, 1919 (a study of the Chicago not of 1919). Negro Hist Bul 30:123-25 My '62

Views of a Negro during "the red summer" of 1919. J of Negro Hist 51:209-218 Jl '66

Detroit

Addenda: Detroit. Editorial. Freedomways 7:198 Summer '67

Detroit's moment of truth. Freedomways 7:354-357 Fall '67

President Johnson's proclamation and executive orders on law and order in the state of Michigan, given verbatim. Race Rela L R 12:1664-1667 Fall '67

East St. Louis, Illinois, 1917

The man who could recite the second inaugural. Freedomways 9:251-256 Summer '69

Harlem 1964

United States Court of Appeals rejects petition of eight Negroes for removal of their cases to the federal court since Negroes and Puerto Ricans were excluded from the grand jury. Race Rela L R 12:352-357 Spring '67

Los Angeles, California

Education level and perceptions of Los Angeles Negroes of educational conditions in a riot area. J of Negro Educ 36:377-384 Fall '67

The fire that time (the Watts riot of 1965) New South 20: 3-5 N '65

Los Angeles, 1965

The McCone Commission and social science. Phylon 29:167-181 2nd q Summer '68

Report from Los Angeles, the Watts riot of 1965. J of Intergroup Rela 5:27-40 Autumn '66

Some lessons from Watts by Bayard Rustin. J of Intergroup Rela 5:41-48 Autumn '66

Miami, Florida

Violence in Miami: one more warning. Summer 23:28-37 Fall '68

Rac

Figure 23. Index to Periodical Articles By and About Blacks

pages to wade through. Sometimes the titles of articles have been shortened so much that they turn out to be ambiguous or misleading. Of course, having only the beginning page is a nuisance, because you generally get more out of a long article than a short one, and *C.R.I.S.* does not tell which to pursue on that account.

Using the *Social Sciences Citation Index*

An exceedingly important source for your literature search is the *Social Sciences Citation Index* (Philadelphia:

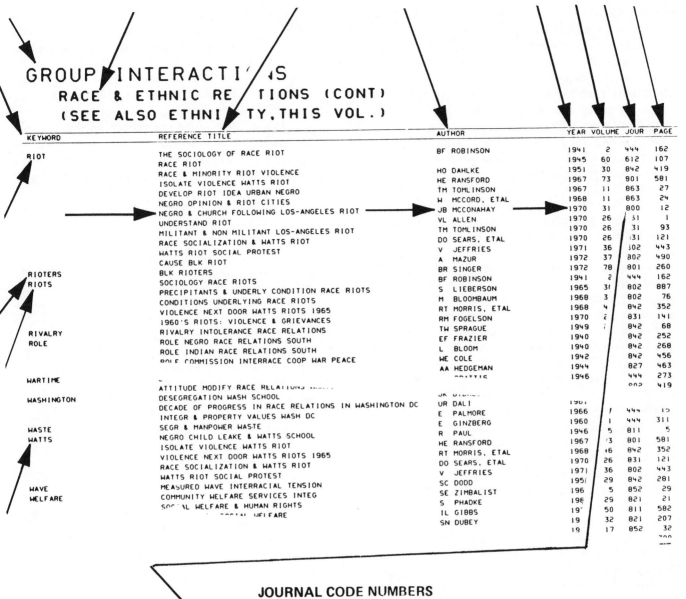

JOURNAL CODE NUMBERS

SOCIOLOGY JOURNALS

800 Sociological Analysis [UK]
801 American Journal of Sociology
802 American Sociological Review
803 American Sociologist
804 Autonomous Groups
805 Berkeley Journal of Sociology
806 British Journal of Criminology [UK]
807 British Journal of Delinquency [UK]
808 British Journal of Psychiatric Social Work [UK]
809 British Journal of Sociology [UK]
810 Canadian Welfare [Canada]
811 Child Welfare
812 Contributions to Indian Sociology [India]
813 Crime and Delinquency
815 Duquesne Review
816 Family Coordinator
817 Human Factors
818 Human Organization
819 Human Relations
820 Impact of Science on Society [France]
821 Indian Journal of Social Work [India]

Figure 24. C.R.I.S.; The Combined Retrospective Index Set to Journals in Sociology, 1895--1974

Institute for Scientific Information, 1972–), which is based on the principle of "citation indexing." A citation index reports articles, books, and other publications being cited and tells which periodical articles cite them in their bibliographies or footnotes. This allows you to pursue the idea in a book or article bibliographically in recent periodicals. The bibliography in the original book or article could only lead you to older materials.

Each issue of the *Social Sciences Citation Index* consists of three separate indexes: a Source Index which provides a complete author index to some 1,000 social sciences periodicals along with the full bibliographical data on each citing article; a Citation Index which lists by author all articles, books, and theses cited by the authors of the articles in the Source Index; and a Permuterm Subject Index which provides a subject approach to the articles in the Source Index. This is done by computerized pairing of each significant word or phrase. Each annual volume has more than a million such word pairs. Both the Permuterm Subject Index and the Citation Index lead the user to the names of authors in the Source Index where full bibliographical information appears. Some special features are a mailing address for authors in the Source Index, a Corporate Index which lists authors under the organizations with which they are affiliated, and a section of anonymous works. The *Social Sciences Citation Index* covers the literature of the specified calendar year. Its two four-month issues are followed by an annual cumulation. To undertake a search, start with a publication you have identified as being central to your interest. Then go to the Citation Index and look for the author of that publication. When you locate the author's name, check to see which of several possible references fits the particular one you are interested in. Under the year, followed by the book title or the journal, volume, and page number for your particular reference, you discover who has currently cited this particular work. Once you have noted the bibliographic citations of the authors who are citing the work with which you started, turn to the Source Index and note the complete bibliographic data for the works you have found.

Let's say that in your reading you have found an article written by Spilerman entitled "Causes of Racial Disturbances" and published in the *American Sociological Review* in 1970. To determine what other work has been done in this particular area, go to the Citation Index, as shown in FIGURE 25, and look under the author's name, Spilerman, and identify the article. Indented under this particular citation is a reference to a work by Vanderza, J.W., that appeared in "SOCIOL Q," which is decoded in the yellow pages of the first volume as *Sociological Quarterly*. Then you look under Vanderza, J.W. in the Source Index. Here you see the title of the journal article that was doing the citing in the Citation Index, followed by the complete information: journal title, volume number, the first page of the article, and the year: "Sociological studies of American Blacks" in *Sociological Quarterly*, volume 14, page 32, 1973. The Source Index also indicates that the address of Vanderza is: Ohio State University, Columbus, Ohio.

It is wise to be highly specific when starting a citation search. Later the search can be expanded in order to build a more extensive bibliography for a particular inquiry. For example, having found a number of source articles, the searcher can use the bibliographies of one or several of these as other entries into the Citation Index. Since authors frequently write more than one closely related paper, additional articles by the author of the first starting reference can also be used as entry points and citations to those articles can be examined to obtain additional bibliography. The Source Index itself may yield relevant current articles by a given author, even though you couldn't find them through the Citation Index because they may not cite any of the known starting sources.

The fundamental question you can answer quickly through the *Social Sciences Citation Index* is: where and by whom has this paper been cited in recent periodical articles? *Social Sciences Citation Index* allows you to determine whether a work has been applied, reviewed, or criticized by others. *SSCI* also enables you to identify social scientists currently working on special problems.

If you do not know a specific author by which to enter the Citation Index or the Source Index, then use the Permuterm Subject Index. As FIGURE 25 shows, this matches significant words from titles of articles, such as "riot," "rioting," and "riots," with other significant words. (Prepositions, articles, etc. are omitted.) Here you see that "Fireston, J M" wrote an article with the words "riots" and "causes" in the title. From here you go to the Source Index and discover fuller bibliographic data. The title of the article is shown to be "Underlying Causes of Urban Riots," the abbreviation of the periodical title is Gen Syst, the volume number is 19, the first page of the article is 117, and the article has 59 references, all shown in abbreviated form. The author's last name is "Firestone" instead of "Fireston"; the computer only prints out ten letters for the author.

Using the *New York Times Index*

Newspapers are invaluable sources of information for current events and for historical data as well. One way to overcome the problem of accessibility to the staggering accumulation of articles is to use the *New York Times Index* (New York: New York Times, 1851–). It is published semimonthly with an annual cumulation which at the present time appears approximately eight months after the end of the year. It is arranged chronologically under subjects and has brief summaries of the articles, along with a reference to the date, page, and column in the paper. Many times the index has enough information to answer a particular question so that it is unnecessary to go to the *New York Times* itself. The comprehensiveness of this newspaper and the thoroughness of the index make it a valuable research aid. Many libraries have back issues of the *Times* on microfilm.

As FIGURE 26 shows, the broad subject heading, "Negroes," is subdivided by particular cities, where you find

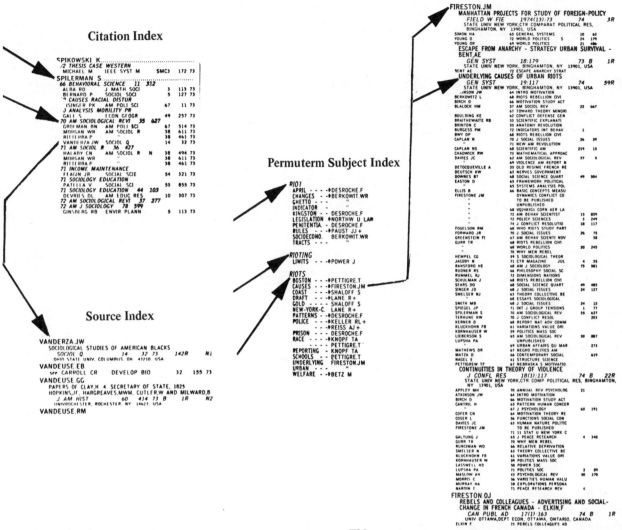

Figure 25. Reprinted from the Social Sciences Citation Index^{TM}, 1973 Annual. Copyright © 1974 by the Institute for Scientific Information.

"Los Angeles" with a chronological summary of articles on the Watts riot. The date, page, and column number are given at the end of the news summary in abbreviated form. "Ag 13. 1:3" stands for August 13, page 1, column 3. The year is not given because the whole volume covers just one year, in this case 1965. The major news stories are shown by bold print.

Finding Pamphlets

Pamphlets can also be helpful sources of recent information or opinion. A pamphlet usually deals with only one subject. Like periodicals and newspapers, when pamphlets are not sources of current information, they serve as histori-

cal sources because they indicate the trend or opinion at a particular time. Libraries organize pamphlets in several ways. Some are cataloged and shelved in the general collection; others are listed in the card catalog but arranged in a filing cabinet by classification numbers. Still others may be filed by subject in cabinets called the Pamphlet File. In this case, there is usually a separate catalog or listing of the subject headings used, on or near the filing cabinets. You will need to find out how pamphlets are arranged in your library.

Searching by Computer

The information available in *Sociological Abstracts,*

31

¶129—*Los Angeles, Calif, Race Riots; National Guard Troops Called Out; Curfew Proclaimed*
Hundreds of Negroes riot in Watts area, Los Angeles, after arrest of Negro drunken driving suspect by hwy patrolmen; all available police units called out as hundreds of persons gather at scene, many throwing rocks; 1 woman hospitalized, Ag 12, 15:3; **100 police and over 300 deputy sheriffs seal off 20-block area as 5,000 Negroes again riot;** map; 200-300 youths fire on police and attack whites, burning cars and throwing debris; 3 persons reptd shot, including TV cameraman; most of injured apparently Negroes and most damage confined to Negro stores and cars; officials unable to explain rioting; Police Chief Parker blames 'young hoodlums,' says violence must be expected 'when you keep telling people they are unfairly treated'; police seeking Natl Guard aid, Ag 13.1:3; **2,000 Natl Guardsmen enter Los Angeles as rioting and looting flares again;** illus; map of area; troops under orders to use rifles, machine guns, tear gas and bayonets in support of 900 local law officers; troops and police open fire on rioters; 4 persons killed, 108 police and civilians injured and 249 rioters arrested; guard spokesman says thousands more troops are on way; violence spreads to San Pedro and San Fernando Valley as gangs of Negroes enter areas; officials rept they have abandoned efforts to halt fire sweeping 3-block section in Watts area; fire dept lists damage at over $10 million; most stores in area believed owned by whites; scores of homeowners and apt dwellers seek evacuation as rioting continues into white areas; police urge residents to remain in homes; police and TV-radio station helicopters fired on repeatedly by Negroes; Parker calls melee 'guerilla warfare'; Mayor Yorty says it may be several days before situation is in complete control; blames riots on 'criminal element'; D Gregory among wounded; shot in thigh while seeking to quell mob; several cases of Negroes saving lives of white victims reptd; Caths United for Racial Equality, RC orgn, urges Pope Paul VI oust Cardinal McIntyre for 'contributing to racial outbursts'; McIntyre comments, Ag 14,1:8; Negro leaders make radio appeals urging end of riots; Negro whose arrest started riots pleads guilty to drunken driving charge, Munic Ct; experts divided on rioting cause; area still tense; Natl Guard comdr Lt Gen Hill says troops will use 'whatever force is necessary' to quell rioting, news conf; says there are no orders to shoot to kill; Lt Gov Anderson called out guard after request from

Parker; Parker critical of delay in approving request; says police did not do job properly in quelling rioting; blames 'half-hearted acquiescence' with civil rights leaders who said situation would cool off if left alone; says police force is not large enough to cope with widespread riot situation; Parker biog; Los Angeles Times Negro ad repr eyewitness account of riot; Gov Brown returning from vacation, Greece, aboard USAF plane sent by Pres Johnson, Ag 14,8:2,4-8; **Lt Gov Anderson proclaims curfew over 35-sq-ml area as violence continues;** illus; maps; Hill says number of troops called up

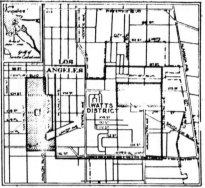

now totals 20,000; calls situation 'mess and getting progressively worse'; 21 persons killed, 600 injured and 1,400 arrested thus far; damage set at $30 million-$100 million; group of Negro civil rights and ch leaders urge martial law, claiming bands of Negroes plan to extend violence into white suburbs; football game and circus canceled because of proximity to area; FAA advises commercial airlines detour area because of continued sniping; 3 major dept stores close their dist branches; Negro merchants display signs in their windows saying 'Negro owned' or 'Blood Brother'; 110 Negroes arrested in racial outburst at nearby Compton, Ag 15,1:8; **Pres Johnson calls riots 'tragic and shocking,' statement, Tex ranch;** warns rioters that their demands can not be won and their grievances remedied through violence';

appeals for all in positions of leadership, Los Angeles, to restore order; orders Pres special counsel L C White and Commerce Under Sec Collins to meet with and aid Gov Brown, Ag 15,1:4; **text,** Ag 15,77:3; observers cite discontent and hate as riot factors; NAACP worker blames 'young hoods and agitators' but notes many others were just discontent and took advantage of situation for emotional release; says he saw Black Muslims in area preaching resistance; Parker bars meeting with anyone speaking for rioters, news conf, Ag 15,1:6; **Brown arrives in Los Angeles; vows to 'restore law and order,' news conf;** earlier held talks with Anderson and other state officials aboard plane shortly after landing; says he does not plan to accept Johnson's offer of Fed help; plans tour of riot area; earlier held talks, NY, with Collins and White; comments on situation, ints, NY, Rome and Athens, Ag 15,1:7; Rev Dr King backs 'full force of police power' to quell riots but warns action can bring only temporary solution; urges massive Negro aid program, Ag 15,66:2; riots cause Negro maid shortage, Ag 15,74:1; riot illus, Ag 15,p78; R Wilkins says he has no plans to send repr to Los Angeles but will rely on NAACP branch there to handle situation; Parker charges Negro 'pseudo-leaders' with trying to fasten blame for Negro crimes upon police, TV int; charges Negro leaders fail to lead; riot scene described; riots given TV coverage; fire dept officer says all dept can do is to keep flames in riot area from spreading; cites lack of manpower; Chief Brunetti says over 550 fire incidents have been reptd in last 2 days, Ag 15,79:2,4,5,7,8; jet airliner skirts riot area, Ag 15,80:4; L Lomax says he will urge Los Angeles Negro leaders to demand Fed mediating teams to help re-establish communication between Negro leaders and city officials; relations between Parker and state officials seen nearing open warfare over delay in sending Natl Guard troops; 40 Negro mins meet with Anderson demanding martial law be declared; charge Parker refused to meet with them and that police officer treated their repr discourteously; other officials and civil rights leaders divided on riot blame; Los Angeles Times ed urges stern measures to end rioting; looting suspect arrested for carrying pair of stolen handcuffs, Ag 15,81:1,8; riot revd; causes cited; illus, Ag 15,IV,1:1; ed cites legacy of Negro deprivation as causes of riots; cites Pres Johnson's s, Howard U, warning of 'destructive rebellion against fabric of soc'; urges speedy nationwide effort to root out factors of soc injustice, Ag 15,IV,8:1

Figure 26. The New York Times Index

Social Sciences Index, and the *New York Times Index*, as well as many other current indexing and abstracting services, has been put into the vast memory of the computer. If your library offers a computer search service you will be able to search many titles that are computerized. In addition, the computer will enable you to make your search more precise than if you used the usual method. If you were searching *Sociological Abstracts* without the computer, you would need to read through all the citations under "Riots —s, —ing" and pick out the relevant ones. A complete search in 1978 would require looking in twenty-five volumes. In contrast, the computer could search a number of volumes at once and could search two or more subject headings at the same time. It would print, for example, only the articles which have both the subject headings "Riot —s, —ing" and "Los Angeles" or "Watts." To get this kind of service you will need to explain your search to someone who knows how to communicate with the computer. If you have a difficult search, ask your reference librarian whether computer assistance is available.

Conclusion

The importance of periodicals, newspapers, and pamphlets cannot be overemphasized in your search for sociological information, because the most recent, up-to-date material on a subject will be found in these sources. Subjects too new, too obscure, or too temporary to be covered by books are often treated in these sources. As you have seen, knowledge of the specialized indexes covering these sources will help you to obtain their valuable information.

Summary

1. The primary reasons for using periodical indexes are to locate recently published articles and to supplement the book collection.
2. The first place to look for recent sociology articles is the *Social Sciences Index*.
3. Next use *Sociological Abstracts* which provides sum-

maries of about 2,000 articles and 250 books per year.

4. Three other sources which cover periodicals of interest to sociologists are: *Public Affairs Information Service Bulletin, Index to Periodicals by and about Blacks,* and *Human Resources Abstracts.*

5. *C.R.I.S.; The Combined Retrospective Index Set to Journals in Sociology, 1895--1975* is a time-saver, but be aware of its weaknesses.

6. The *Social Sciences Citations Index* tells where a particular book or article has been cited in some 1,000 periodicals. It also has a subject approach based on significant words from the titles of articles.

7. The *New York Times Index* has brief summaries of articles in one of the country's leading newspapers and tells where the complete article can be found.

8. Pamphlets also supply current information.

9. The computer may be able to help you with a long or difficult search.

No society has ever been found without a government.
Stuart Chase

The United States government issues a great amount of sociological information in the form of government reports, investigations, statistical compilations, and other types of publications. The United States government is the largest publisher in the world. Its abundant financial resources allow it to publish materials on a wide variety of subjects, from corn oil production to Congressional committee hearings on violence. One reason the government needs all these publications is to help it in its decision making processes.

The most useful collections of United States government documents are found in the more than 900 "depository libraries," which are designated by the Superintendent of Documents. These libraries regularly receive, free of cost, any document published in a previously selected series or category. If a library is a "complete depository" it will receive almost all items printed at the government printing office; if it is a "selective depository" it will get only a selection of titles. If your particular library does not happen to be a depository you can borrow materials from one nearby. Ask your librarian.

Although government documents are both invaluable and available, many students of sociology never discover them. This is because of a lack of knowledge about the kinds of publications available and the procedures for locating them. Government documents are overlooked because they are generally not cataloged with the books and they are

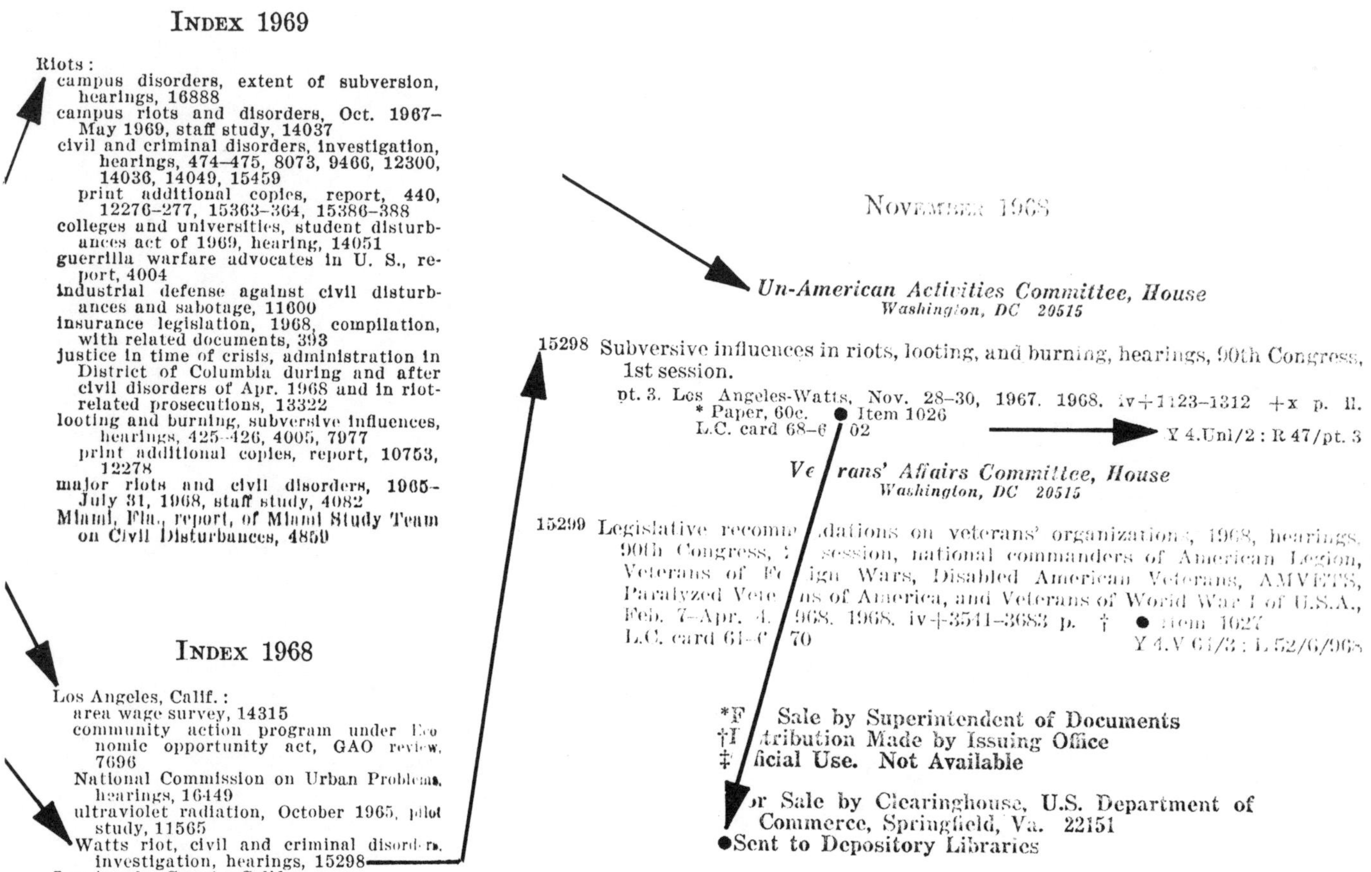

INDEX 1969

Riots:
campus disorders, extent of subversion, hearings, 16888
campus riots and disorders, Oct. 1967–May 1969, staff study, 14037
civil and criminal disorders, investigation, hearings, 474–475, 8073, 9466, 12300, 14036, 14049, 15459
print additional copies, report, 440, 12276–277, 15363–364, 15386–388
colleges and universities, student disturbances act of 1969, hearing, 14051
guerrilla warfare advocates in U. S., report, 4004
industrial defense against civil disturbances and sabotage, 11600
insurance legislation, 1968, compilation, with related documents, 393
justice in time of crisis, administration in District of Columbia during and after civil disorders of Apr. 1968 and in riot-related prosecutions, 13322
looting and burning, subversive influences, hearings, 425–426, 4005, 7977
print additional copies, report, 10753, 12278
major riots and civil disorders, 1965–July 31, 1968, staff study, 4082
Miami, Fla., report, of Miami Study Team on Civil Disturbances, 4850

INDEX 1968

Los Angeles, Calif.:
area wage survey, 14315
community action program under Economic opportunity act, GAO review, 7696
National Commission on Urban Problems, hearings, 16449
ultraviolet radiation, October 1965, pilot study, 11565
Watts riot, civil and criminal disorders, investigation, hearings, 15298
Los Angeles County, Calif.:

NOVEMBER 1968

Un-American Activities Committee, House
Washington, DC 20515

15298 Subversive influences in riots, looting, and burning, hearings, 90th Congress, 1st session.
pt. 3. Los Angeles-Watts, Nov. 28–30, 1967. 1968. iv+1123–1312 +x p. il.
* Paper, 60c. ● Item 1026
L.C. card 68–60302 Y 4.Un1/2 : R 47/pt. 3

Veterans' Affairs Committee, House
Washington, DC 20515

15299 Legislative recommendations on veterans' organizations, 1968, hearings, 90th Congress, 2d session, national commanders of American Legion, Veterans of Foreign Wars, Disabled American Veterans, AMVETS, Paralyzed Veterans of America, and Veterans of World War I of U.S.A., Feb. 7–Apr. 4, 1968. 1968. iv+3541–3683 p. † ● Item 1027
L.C. card 61–60770 Y 4.V 64/3 : L 52/6/968

*For Sale by Superintendent of Documents
†Distribution Made by Issuing Office
‡Official Use. Not Available
For Sale by Clearinghouse, U.S. Department of Commerce, Springfield, Va. 22151
●Sent to Depository Libraries

Figure 27. Monthly Catalog of United States Government Publications usually shelved separately from the books and periodicals.

The most important source for locating government documents is a bibliography entitled the *Monthly Catalog of United States Government Publications* (Washington, DC: U.S. Government Printing Office, 1885–). This is a monthly list of publications issued by all branches of the government. Before 1974, the *Monthly Catalog* had only a subject index. Now it has indexes for authors, titles, and subjects.

To use the *Monthly Catalog* for your sample topic, consult the annual index under the subject, "riots," and also under the city, "Los Angeles," where there are lists of abbreviated titles followed by entry numbers. As FIGURE 27 shows, one of these abbreviated titles reads "Watts riot, civil and criminal disorders investigation, hearings, 15298." Looking up this number in the main section of the *Monthly Catalog*, you find a full description of the document. Here you see that the House Un-American Activities Committee (centered on the page in bold print) issued the 203-page document, and its Superintendent of Documents classification number is Y4.Un1/2:R47/pt.3. If your library is typical and arranges its government documents by the Superintendent of Documents classification number you can use this to locate the particular document on the library shelves. Before July 1976 and after March 1977 the *Monthly Catalog* indicates which documents are available to depository libraries by the placement of a large black dot near the title of the item. Between those dates depository items are indicated by the fact that an item number is mentioned along with other bibliographical information.

Not all libraries organize government documents in the same way. When you are trying to locate documents for the first time, it is wise to ask for assistance so that you do not overlook any pertinent documents and so that you learn the arrangement of the documents in your particular library. Government documents are sometimes cataloged and shelved like other library materials, according to the Dewey Decimal classification or the Library of Congress classification. In this case the card catalog is used to locate items by issuing agencies and titles. Sometimes government documents are classified and cataloged like other library materials but kept in a special file or section of shelves. In this case, "Government Documents" or "Govt. Doc." will be added to the call number. The documents may also be arranged on the shelves alphabetically by issuing body, with a separate catalog. Probably the most common system is for documents to be arranged according to the Superintendent of Documents classification number in a separate collection with a separate catalog. Some libraries use a combination of the above mentioned techniques for different portions of their collection of government publications, depending on their type and frequency of use.

Summary

1. The U.S. government issues many publications useful to students of sociology.
2. The *Monthly Catalog* is the most comlete bibliography of government documents.
3. Government documents are organized in different ways. Most libraries keep them as a separate collection arranged under the Superintendent of Documents classification number.

Do not put your faith in what
statistics say until you have
carefully considered what
they do not say.
William W. Watt.

The generalizations in your writing may be weak unless they are supported with statistics. Fortunately, the United States government collects and disseminates a vast amount of statistical data, as was stressed in Chapter 7.

Sources of United States Statistics

Probably the best place to begin a search for national, state, and local statistics is the *Statistical Abstract of the United States* (Washington, DC: U.S. Government Printing Office, 1879–) which is prepared annually by the U.S. Bureau of the Census. This book includes a summary of the most important statistics on the social, political, economic, and cultural activities of the United States. It covers such topics as population, immigration, vital statistics, education, science, law enforcement, and communications. Each section is prefaced with an essay designed to introduce the tables which follow. This book also serves as a guide to other statistical publications and sources; under each table in the book is reported the source of the data, which usually leads to more detailed statistics. FIGURE 28 shows that you begin to use this guide by turning to the subject index in the back of the book and looking under the subject heading "riots." Then examine the pages which are cited. Turning to page 151 in the main section, you find a table listing grievances in cities where the riots occurred. At the bottom of the table is reported the source of the data. In this case, it is the March 1968 *Report* of the National Advisory Committee on Civil Disorders. The *Monthly Catalog* for 1968 will help locate this report with its more detailed statistics.

Another statistical handbook issued by the U.S. Bureau of the Census is the *County and City Data Book* (Washington, DC: U.S. Government Printing Office, 1949–), which has been published six times and provides tables of local and regional statistics. Statistics are included for cities, counties, standard metropolitan areas, and urbanized areas. Figures are given for such topics as education, population characteristics, business, industry, government, housing, and vital statistics. For example, you can use the *County and City Data Book* to look up a city of 25,000 or more and see what percentage of the families have incomes less than $3,000 per year.

Another useful source of numerical data is Paul Wasserman's *Statistics Sources*, 5th ed. (Detroit: Gale Research, 1977). This is a subject list of sources of current statistics. The emphasis is on U.S. national publications and organiza-

tions. Very brief annotations are given. There is no listing under the subject heading "riots" but under the subject heading, "civil disorders," the same March 1968 *Report* of the National Advisory Commission on Civil Disorders is given as a source of statistical data.

The *American Statistics Index* (Washington, DC: Congressional Information Service, 1973–) is a comprehensive guide to federal statistics. The basic volume indexes and abstracts all the federal statistical publications available on January 1, 1973, and includes all of the major statistical output of the previous decade. Monthly issues up-date the basic volume and are cumulated annually. The objective of this publication is to abstract all U.S. government publications "which contain statistical data of probable research significance."

Note in FIGURE 29 that the index to subjects and names has a heading, "Riots and disorders," which refers to six sources of statistics. To find "Civil disorders, summer 1967, Natl Advisory Commission rept, supplementary studies," you look at abstract number 14898–2, as indicated. When you get to this abstract, you find, as in FIGURE 29, that it supplies full bibliographic data, including the Superintendent of Documents number. Note that pages 3 to 67 have 76 tables of statistics describing the uses of violence, along with other topics.

Sources of International Statistics

Of all the international organizations that compile and disseminate statistics one of the largest and most productive is the United Nations. Two of the United Nations' major statistical publications are the *Statistical Yearbook* (New York: United Nations, 1948–), and the *Demographic Yearbook* (New York: United Nations, 1948–). It turns out that U.N. statistics aren't very relevant for our sample topic, but they will be for other topics.

The *Statistical Yearbook*, appearing annually, is a primary source for international statistics on population, manpower, health, vital statistics, wages and prices, housing, and education. The material is arranged by subject and indexed by country. Special tables illustrate important economic developments.

The *Demographic Yearbook* is also published annually and presents detailed information on selected demographic characteristics, such as natality, mortality, population distribution, population trends, marriage and divorce, and

Index

Page

Revolvers. *See* Firearms.
Rhode Island. *See* State data.
Rhodesia. *See* Foreign countries.
Rice:
    Acreage and value 606,607
    Consumption 87
    Farm sales under price supports 597
    Foreign trade 604,605,611,784
    Prices 353,607
    Production 604,606,607,611
       Foreign countries 819
       World 802
    Shopper's expenditure for 360
Rifles, production and imports 150
Riots (civil disturbances) 148,151
Rivers, canals, harbors, etc.:
    Commerce, domestic and foreign 565,572,574,575
    Federal expenditures for 576
    Lengths of principal rivers 173
Roads, public. *See* Highways.

Assassinations—Grievances—Arrests   151

No. 240. Political Assassinations and Assaults: 1835 to 1968

[Assault defined as any attack on persons holding political office or any individuals or groups of individuals for political reasons. Rates based on averages of appropriate decennial census figures. For composition of regions, see fig. I, p. xii]

REGION	Number	Rate per million population	PERIOD	Number	Rate per million population
United States, 1835–1968...	81	(X)	1835–1864	3	(Z)
			1865–1894	43	0.03
Northeast	7	0.02	1895–1924	12	(Z)
Southeast	28	0.18	1925–1934	3	0.02
North Central	11	0.03	1935–1944	4	0.03
South Central	25	0.13	1945–1954	[1]11	0.07
West	10	0.10	1955–1968	5	0.03

X Not applicable.   Z Less than 0.005 percent.   [1] Includes 5 Congressmen shot in 1954 in a single attack.

Source: National Commission on the Causes and Prevention of Violence, *Task Force Report on Assassinations*, 1969.

No. 241. Grievances in Cities Where Civil Disorders Occurred: 1967

[Based on surveys made in 20 cities where civil disorders occurred. Grievances evaluated as to significance in each city and rank and points assigned to the 4 most serious, as follows: 4 points for 1st place, 3 for 2d, 2 for 3d, and 1 for 4th. Total points for each grievance category represents number of cities in which it was ranked among the top 4 multiplied by the number of points. Thus, a 4-point grievance assigned to 2 cities amounted to 8 points. Judgments of severity based on frequency of mention of a particular grievance, relative intensity with which it was discussed, references to incidents exemplifying it, and estimates of severity]

GRIEVANCE CATEGORY	Cities[1]	Points	GRIEVANCE CATEGORY	Cities[1]	Points
Police practices	14	45.5	Disrespectful white attitudes	4	6.5
Unemployment, underemployment	17	42.0	Discriminatory admin. of justice	3	4.5
Inadequate housing	14	36.0	Inadequate Federal programs	1	2.5
Inadequate education	9	21.0			
Poor recreation facilities	8	21.0	Inadequate municipal services	1	2.0
Ineffective political structure and grievance mechanisms	5	14.0	Discriminatory consumer and credit practices	2	2.0

[1] Where grievances were mentioned as significant.

Source: The National Advisory Commission on Civil Disorders, *Report*, March 1968.

Figure 28. Statistical Abstract of the United States

14898-2 **SUPPLEMENTAL STUDIES FOR THE NATIONAL ADVISORY COMMISSION ON CIVIL DISORDERS**
July 1968. viii+248 p.
●Item 851-J. GPO $1.50.
ASI/MF Pr36.8:C49/St9.
16461(68). 68-62329.

Report presenting 3 supplemental independent studies conducted under the Commission's auspices on racial attitudes in American cities and on participation in the 1967 riots.

Contents:

a. Campbell, Angus; and Schuman, Howard, "Racial Attitudes in Fifteen American Cities"Survey Research Center, University of Michigan, June 1968. Study funded by the Ford Foundation and derived from sample survey data. Covers black views of racial issues, white beliefs about Negroes, comparison of black and white attitudes and experiences in the city, and uses of violence, with 76 tables. (p. 3-67)

b. Rossi, Peter (et al.), "Between White and Black, Faces of American Institutions in the Ghetto"Johns Hopkins University, June 1968. Study funded by the Ford Foundation and derived from sample surv— tudes and experie— ..etail mer- groups in ¹ᵉ ..elfare workers, and ...cans, with 90 tables. (p. 69-

c. Fogelson, Robert M.; and Hill, Robert B., "Who Riots? A Study of Participation in the 1967 Riots"MIT, July 1968. Study funded by the Commission and derived from a combination of sample surveys and arrest data. Study covers methodological problems, extent of participation, composition of rioters, and sentiment of the Negro community, with 24 tables. (p. 217-248)

14898-3 **FIREARMS, VIOLENCE, AND CIVIL DISORDERS**
July 1968. vii ⁝ ⁝
† Stan᷄

Index by Subjects and Names

Riots and disorders
  Civil disorders, summer 1967, firearms use in Newark and Detroit, Natl Advisory Commission special study, 14898-3
  Civil disorders, summer 1967, Natl Advisory Commission rpt, 14898-1
  Civil disorders, summer 1967, Natl Advisory Commission rpt, supplementary studies, 14898-2
  Detroit riot, July 1967, profile of 500 black prisoners, 6408-4
  Insurance programs, Fed Insurance Admin, 1968 rpt, 25248-1.10
  Natl Guard emergency activations, by State, FY72, annual rpt, 3704-3

Figure 29. American Statistics Index

---

ethnic and economic characteristics. The material is also arranged by subject and indexed by country.

These then are a few basic sources to get you started in your search for statistics. Because statistics are often quoted in periodical articles, in pamphlets and in books, the various bibliographies and indexes mentioned throughout this guide will also lead you to needed statistics.

Summary

1. Statistics are needed to support some generalizations.

2. The *Statistical Abstract* summarizes many government statistics useful to students of sociology and tells where the complete statistics can be found.

3. The *County and City Data Book* has tables of local and regional statistics.

4. *Statistics Sources* is a subject bibliography for sources of statistics.

5. The *American Statistics Index* indexes U.S. government publications which have statistical data.

6. The United Nations issues the *Statistical Year Book* and the *Demographic Yearbook*, which report statistics on many countries.

Man has a taxonomic urge, a desire to classify and define. Kenneth R. Muse.

As you read, you may come across concepts that you need to define. Almost all students are familiar with an unabridged dictionary, such as Webster's, which, like all dictionaries, is a book about words, their historical development, and varied meanings. What you may not know is that there are many dictionaries devoted to many specialized subjects, such as psychology, battles, and plants.

In the field of sociology, there are several excellent dictionaries. Some, such as *Elsevier's Dictionary of Criminal Science in Eight Languages*, 1960, or the *Multilingual Demographic Dictionary*, 1958, are so highly specialized that they are seldom used by undergraduates or masters candidates. There are three *general* dictionaries of sociology which these students should use heavily because they are so basic to the study of sociology.

Henry Fairchild's *Dictionary of Sociology* (New York: Philosophical Library, 1944) very briefly defines some 500 terms, including race conflict, race prejudice, race relations, and racism.

Thomas Ford Hoult's *Dictionary of Modern Sociology* (Totowa, NJ: Littlefield, Adams, 1969) reflects current usage and often supplies a recent quotation. As FIGURE 30 shows, the definition of racism includes a quotation from Malcolm X, along with "also see" references to "apartheid" and "white man's burden."

Geoffrey Mitchell's *Dictionary of Sociology* (Chicago: Aldine, 1968) is a selection of less than 250 of the most important terms, but its definitions are fuller than those in the two dictionaries described above and it features references to further reading. For example, FIGURE 31 shows an extended definition of anomie and refers to two books which treat this term. Mitchell's work also has biographical sketches of leading sociologists, such as Emile Durkheim and C. Wright Mills.

Summary

1. Dictionaries are useful for defining words.
2. Three dictionaries cover sociological terms.

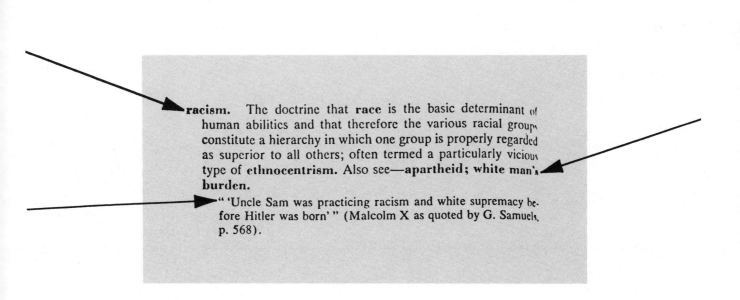

racism. The doctrine that **race** is the basic determinant of human abilities and that therefore the various racial groups constitute a hierarchy in which one group is properly regarded as superior to all others; often termed a particularly vicious type of **ethnocentrism.** Also see—**apartheid; white man's burden.**
" 'Uncle Sam was practicing racism and white supremacy before Hitler was born' " (Malcolm X as quoted by G. Samuels, p. 568).

Figure 30. Dictionary of Modern Sociology

anomic: anomy. The term *anomie* was first used by the French sociologist, Émile Durkheim, to refer to several aspects of social participation where the conditions necessary for man to fulfil himself and to attain happiness were not present. These conditions were that conduct should be governed by norms, that these norms should form an integrated and non-conflicting system, that the individual should be morally involved with other people so that 'the image of the one who completes me becomes inseparable from mine' and so that clear limits were set to the pleasures attainable in life. Any state where there are unclear, conflicting or unintegrated norms, in which the individual had no morally significant relations with others or in which there were no limits set to the attainment of pleasure was a state of *anomie*.

R. K. Merton uses the term to refer to a state in which socially prescribed goals and the norms governing their attainment are incompatible. Leo Srole has attempted to construct an index of *anomie*. In most attempts to make *anomie* measurable, emphasis is placed on lack of clarity in goals and norms or upon the absence of social ties. All such attempts involve a more restricted use of the concept than Durkheim's which was related to a philosophical conception of human nature. See E. Durkheim, *Division of Labour*; translated 1947, *Suicide*, translated 1951. R. K. Merton, *Social Theory and Social Structure*, 1949, ch. IV.

J.R.

Figure 31. Dictionary of Sociology

It is rendering mutual service to men of virtue and understanding to make them acquainted with one another. Thomas Jefferson, *Writings*.

Why Use a Guide?

Right now you are reading a selective guide to the basic references in sociology, but it may not include everything you need to know. You may require a more comprehensive guide because you need more specialized reference sources for your topic. Guides to the literature of a subject map the way through the literature, and by so doing, they help to introduce, organize, and evaluate material. This distinguishes guides from bibliographies (whether annotated or not) and from introductory treatises. A guide is more versatile and more informative than a bibliography, and unlike the treatises, it introduces the literature, not the content of the subject. Guides to the literature can lead you to materials in your library and can also alert you to the existence of materials not available in your library.

SOCIAL PROBLEMS

About twenty years ago the Society for the Study of Social Problems was formed to enable social scientists to apply their knowledge to the solution of social problems. The creation of this organization was a protest against the seemingly academic nature of sociology at the time. Today, however, there is some anxiety about a possible disbalance in the opposite direction.

In recent years sociologists have selected several problem areas in which they have contributed to understanding as well as to shaping social policy. Foremost among these is the study of poverty, and under the label "culture of poverty" sociologists have stressed the attitudes, values, and lifestyles that have fostered the isolation of the poor. Empirical research demonstrated the many inequities: the poor were less healthy, physically and mentally, than the rich; they paid more than others for the same goods; they were restricted in occupational opportunities; and they limited their own aspirations. When planning and action agencies were created to deal with these issues, sociologists took active roles. They helped to sharpen goals, formulate ways of reaching low-income families, and evaluate the effectiveness of the programs.

However, it does not appear that their operational work has been fed back into the mainstream of sociological knowledge. It may be, as some have suggested, that taking society's definition of a social problem is not the same as working upon a sociological problem.

E100 Becker, Howard S. Social problems: a modern approach. New York: Wiley, 1966. 770p.

E101 Caplovitz, David. The poor pay more. New York: Free Pr., 1963. 225p.

E102 Frieden, Bernard J., and Robert Morris, eds. Urban planning and social policy. New York: Basic, 1968. 459p.

E103 Gans, Herbert J. People and plans: essays on urban problems and solutions. New York: Basic, 1968. 395p.

E104 Miller, S. M., and P. Roby. The future of inequality. New York: Basic, 1970. 272p.

E105 Reissman, F., and H. I. Popper. Up from poverty: new career ladders for nonprofessionals. New York: Harper, 1968. 332p.

E106 Smigel, Erwin, ed. Handbook on the study of social problems. Chicago: Rand McNally, 1971. 734p.

Figure 32. **Sources of Information in the Social Sciences; A Guide to the Literature**

One of the most comprehensive guides in the social sciences in Carl M. White's *Sources of Information in the Social Sciences; A Guide to the Literature*, 2d ed. Chicago: American Library Association, 1973). It lists the major reference sources as well as treatises in sociology. Other subject areas covered are: anthropology, history, economics, business administration, psychology, education, political science, and law. For each discipline there is a bibliographical essay written by a specialist to explain the history and methodology of the discipline. This is followed by essays and booklists on the various subtopics of the discipline, and annotated lists of reference sources, grouped by form, such as abstracts, bibliographies, encyclopedias, and handbooks. Note in FIGURE 32 that the sociology chapter has a section entitled "Social Problems" which has an essay introducing seven books. The *Handbook on the Study of Social Problems* is cited here because it is one of the basic books on social problems.

Like White's guide, Berthold F. Hoselitz's *A Reader's Guide to the Social Sciences*, rev. ed. (New York: Free Press, 1970) provides a general introduction to the literature of the social sciences. Hoselitz's guide describes the books, journals, pamphlets, and reference books that are used in the major disciplines. Each chapter is devoted to a different discipline: sociology, anthropology, psychology, political science, economics, and geography.

Another very useful guide is Pauline Bart's *Student Sociologist's Handbook* (Cambridge, MA: Schenkman, 1971). This work focuses on the foundations of the discipline and gives the student a broad view of new approaches to sociology. The guide provides a discussion of sociological method, a glossary of statistical terms, a guide to the mechanics of library research, and a description of the techniques of writing a research or field work paper.

How to Use a Guide to General Reference Sources

A comprehensive annotated bibliography of reference sources in English is: Eugene P. Sheehy, *Guide to Reference Books*, 9th ed. (Chicago: American Library Association, 1976). Its twelve-page section on sociology is broken down into five sections, one of which is "Race Relations and Minorities." One of the subsections, shown in FIGURE 33, shows annotations for some of the sixteen bibliographies on Afro-Americans. This would lead a student working on the Watts riot to several new sources, including the *Black Information Index*.

Summary

1. Guides to the literature not only introduce the literature in a specific field but also provide descriptive and evaluative discussions.

Racial and minority groups

Afro-Americans

Bibliography

Black information index. v.1, no.1– . [Herndon, Va., Infonetics], 1970– . Bimonthly.   **CC114**

Designed "to disseminate information by and about black people and their environment."— *Pref.* Bibliographic citations are followed by brief notes on content. Some 80 publications are scanned for pertinent articles. Arrangement is by broad subject categories (e.g., Africa, Education, Housing, Urban and rural issues) with subdivisions as appropriate. There is an index of subjects (mainly personal, place, and corporate names) and an author index.
   Z1361.N39B554

Blacks in America; bibliographical essays, by James M. McPherson [and others]. Garden City, N.Y., Doubleday, 1971. 430p.   **CC115**

". . . an attempt to combine narrative, interpretation, and bibliography in a chronological and topical framework that will provide teachers, students, and interested readers with an up-to-date guide to Afro-American history and culture."—*Pref.* Material is arranged under 100 topical headings, with name and subject index.
   Z1361.N39B56

Dumond, Dwight Lowell. A bibliography of antislavery in America. Ann Arbor, Univ. of Michigan Pr., [1961]. 119p.   **CC116**

Prepared to accompany the author's *Antislavery; the crusade for freedom in America* (1961), "this is the literature written and circulated by those active in the antislavery movement and used by the author."—*Note.* Includes works published up to the time of the Civil War.   Z1249.S6D8

Hampton Institute, Hampton, Va. Collis P. Huntington Library. A classified catalogue of the Negro collection, comp. by the Writers' Program of the Work Projects Administration in the state of Virginia. Sponsored by Hampton Institute. [n.p.], 1940. 255p., [35]p.   **CC117**

More than 5,000 titles on the Negro in Africa and in America. Particularly strong in material on slavery and reconstruction. Classified, with author and title index.   Z1361.N39H3

Howard University, Washington, D.C. Library. Moorland Foundation. Dictionary catalog of the Jesse E. Moorland collection of Negro life and history. Boston, G. K. Hall, 1970. 9v.   **CC118**

Reproduction of the catalog cards of an important collection of more than 105,000 items. Includes entries for selected periodical articles, speeches published in newspapers, etc.

Miller, Elizabeth W. The Negro in America: a bibliography. 2d ed., rev. and enl., comp. by Mary L. Fisher. Cambridge, Harvard Univ. Pr., 1970. 351p.   **CC119**

1st ed. 1966.
A listing of books and periodical articles grouped under such headings as "History," "Intergroup relations," "Urban problems," "Employment," "Education," "Political rights and suffrage," with new sections added in the revised edition to cover music, literature and the arts. Emphasis is on materials published since 1954. Author index. A useful and thorough compilation, and a needed complement to Work's bibliography (CC129).   Z1361.N39M5

Figure 33. Guide to Reference Books

2. Carl White's *Sources of Information in the Social Sciences* and Berthold Hoselitz's *A Reader's Guide to the Social Sciences* are two guides with chapters discussing the literature of sociology.

3. Pauline Bart's *Student Sociologist's Handbook* provides an orientation for students of sociology that covers more than the literature.

4. Eugene Sheehy's *Guide to Reference Books* classifies and describes more than 170 reference sources on sociology.

It is really satisfying to use bibliographies, periodical indexes, and abstracts, when they lead you to vital books and articles in your library. But these reference sources can be frustrating to use if your library does not own the materials you need most. It would not be so frustrating if you did not know that the materials existed! Fortunately, your problem is not insoluble if you act in time.

Your reference librarian may be able to borrow the books you need from another library or may be able to get photocopies of any articles you need. All that is necessary is time, full and accurate information on the item desired and, in case of photocopy, a little money. The time required is generally a minimum of two weeks depending on the availability at other libraries and their backlog of requests. The full information needed generally includes a report of the page where you found the book or article cited. This may seem like bureaucratic red tape, but this information is required by lending libraries and is good insurance against errors in transmission. If you do not have the full bibliographical information (author, title, publisher, place, date, and page) ask your reference librarian to help you find it. The cost of photocopies varies, with a usual minimum of about $2.00. Libraries often make no charge for mailing books, but they seldom mail periodicals.

If you are an undergraduate at a university, you may find that this interlibrary loan service is not available to you, partly because a university library serving doctoral students is presumed to have a collection that is adequate for undergraduates. Interlibrary loan service is more readily available to undergraduates at colleges, which often have made special arrangements to borrow from a nearby university or state library. If another library is nearby, your time is short, or your library will not borrow for you, then you may prefer to visit another library. Your reference librarian can give you the address, phone number, subject specialties, and occasionally the hours of most libraries you may want to visit. Libraries generally let visitors use materials in the library only.

If you need a particular periodical, your reference librarian can help you find which nearby libraries own it. The librarian finds the locations of periodicals by using the *Union List of Serials, New Serials Titles*, and other sources. With a little help, you can do the same. Books are harder to locate, but the *National Union Catalog of the Library of Congress* does give the location of a good many books published 1953 and later. However, if you want to be certain that a particular book is available, you can phone a library and ask them to hold it for you if they find it on the shelf.

Using the *Library of Congress Catalog -- Books: Subjects*

If you are having difficulty finding enough books on your topic, consult the subject-arranged book catalog of the world's largest library: U.S. Library of Congress, *Library of Congress Catalog -- Books: Subjects; A Cumulative List of Works Represented by Library of Congress Printed Cards, 1950--* (Totowa, NJ: Rowman and Littlefield, 1955–). Its five-year cumulations and quarterly supplements are a comprehensive subject listing of books published in the U.S. from 1950 to date. As FIGURE 34 shows, if you look in the 1965–69 volumes under the heading "Los Angeles – Riots, 1965," you see that the source includes, besides a book, a state government document issued by the California Governor's Commission on the Los Angeles Riots and several pamphlets put out by the University of California's Institute of Government and Public Affairs. Such pamphlets and state documents rarely appear in other bibliographies, but they can be found in this most comprehensive of all general subject bibliographies. Many college libraries do not own the *Library of Congress -- Books: Subjects*, which totals over 200 volumes and over one hundred twenty thousand pages, but you may be able to visit a library which does have it. Whatever promising books you find there can be pursued through your own library and elsewhere.

The *International Bibliography of Sociology* (London: Tavistock; Chicago: Aldine, 1952–) is another comprehensive bibliography, but, unlike *Library of Congress -- Books: Subjects*, it covers only sociology. Its annual volumes currently cite more than 5,000 unannotated books, articles, government documents and pamphlets from many countries and in many languages. Its introductory pages, subject headings and subject indexes are in English and French. As FIGURE 35 shows, you can approach it through its subject index and its classification scheme. The broad subject heading, "Race problems," leads to a group of thirty-seven items that can also be found in the classification scheme under "Race relations." "Race problems" also leads to about forty items scattered through the classification. These would not be worth looking up unless you have time for a thorough search. FIGURE 35 shows that the *International Bibliography of Sociology* cites a relevant article by Lieberson in the *American Sociological Review*.

When you visit another library, be sure to check its card

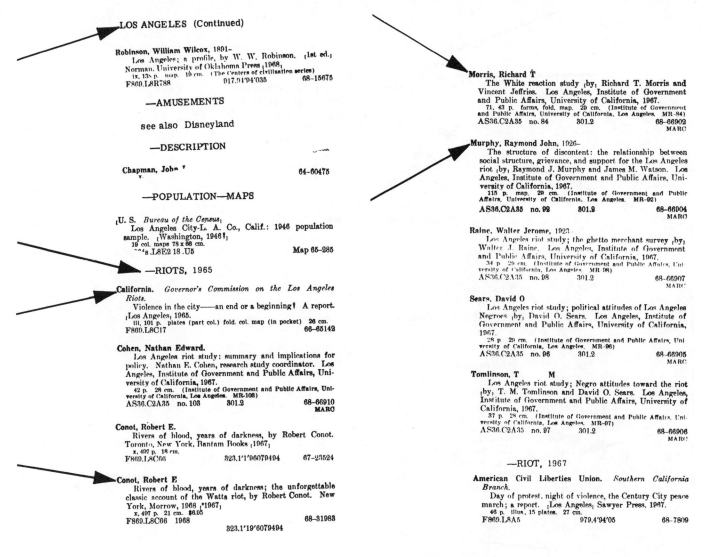

LOS ANGELES (Continued)

Robinson, William Wilcox, 1891–
Los Angeles; a profile, by W. W. Robinson. [1st ed.]
Norman, University of Oklahoma Press [1968]
ix, 135 p. map. 19 cm. (The Centers of civilization series)
F869.L8R788   917.91'94'035   68–15675

—AMUSEMENTS

see also Disneyland

—DESCRIPTION

Chapman, John   64–60475

—POPULATION—MAPS

[U. S. *Bureau of the Census*]
Los Angeles City–L. A. Co., Calif.: 1946 population
sample. [Washington, 1946?]
19 col. maps 78 x 66 cm.
***s.L8E2 18 .U5   Map 65–285

—RIOTS, 1965

California. *Governor's Commission on the Los Angeles
Riots.*
Violence in the city——an end or a beginning? A report.
[Los Angeles] 1965.
iii, 101 p. plates (part col.) fold. col. map (in pocket) 26 cm.
F869.L8C17   66–65142

Cohen, Nathan Edward.
Los Angeles riot study: summary and implications for
policy. Nathan E. Cohen, research study coordinator. Los
Angeles, Institute of Government and Public Affairs, University of California, 1967.
42 p. 28 cm. (Institute of Government and Public Affairs, University of California, Los Angeles. MR–108)
AS36.C2A35 no. 103   301.2   68–66910
                                             MARC

Conot, Robert E.
Rivers of blood, years of darkness, by Robert Conot.
Toronto, New York, Bantam Books [1967]
x, 497 p. 18 cm.
F869.L8C66   323.1'1'96079494   67–23524

Conot, Robert E
Rivers of blood, years of darkness; the unforgettable
classic account of the Watts riot, by Robert Conot. New
York, Morrow, 1968 [*1967]
x, 497 p. 21 cm. $8.95
F869.L8C66 1968   68–31983
                          323.1'19'6079494

Morris, Richard T
The White reaction study [by] Richard T. Morris and
Vincent Jeffries. Los Angeles, Institute of Government
and Public Affairs, University of California, 1967.
71, 43 p. forms, fold. map. 29 cm. (Institute of Government
and Public Affairs, University of California, Los Angeles. MR–84)
AS36.C2A35 no. 84   301.2   68–66902
                                             MARC

Murphy, Raymond John, 1926–
The structure of discontent: the relationship between
social structure, grievance, and support for the Los Angeles
riot [by] Raymond J. Murphy and James M. Watson. Los
Angeles, Institute of Government and Public Affairs, University of California, 1967.
115 p. map. 29 cm. (Institute of Government and Public
Affairs, University of California, Los Angeles. MR–92)
AS36.C2A35 no. 92   301.2   68–66904
                                             MARC

Raine, Walter Jerome, 1923–
Los Angeles riot study; the ghetto merchant survey [by]
Walter J. Raine. Los Angeles, Institute of Government
and Public Affairs, University of California, 1967.
34 p. 29 cm. (Institute of Government and Public Affairs, University of California, Los Angeles. MR–98)
AS36.C2A35 no. 98   301.2   68–66907
                                             MARC

Sears, David O
Los Angeles riot study; political attitudes of Los Angeles
Negroes [by] David O. Sears. Los Angeles, Institute of
Government and Public Affairs, University of California,
1967.
28 p. 29 cm. (Institute of Government and Public Affairs, Uni-
versity of California, Los Angeles. MR–96)
AS36.C2A35 no. 96   301.2   68–66905
                                             MARC

Tomlinson, T   M
Los Angeles riot study; Negro attitudes toward the riot
[by] T. M. Tomlinson and David O. Sears. Los Angeles,
Institute of Government and Public Affairs, University of
California, 1967.
37 p. 28 cm. (Institute of Government and Public Affairs, Uni-
versity of California, Los Angeles. MR–97)
AS36.C2A35 no. 97   301.2   68–66906
                                             MARC

—RIOT, 1967

American Civil Liberties Union. *Southern California
Branch.*
Day of protest. night of violence, the Century City peace
march; a report. [Los Angeles] Sawyer Press, 1967.
46 p. illus. 15 plates. 27 cm.
F869.L8A5   979.4'94'05   68–7809

Figure 34. Library of Congress Catalog --- Books: Subjects

catalog under the subject headings you found useful in your own library. The larger the collection, the more you can expect to find, and you may discover some useful titles you have not seen on a bibliography.

Summary

1. Bibliographies and periodical indexes can be frustrating to use if your library does not own the materials cited.

2. You can ask your reference librarian to borrow books from other libraries or get photocopies of articles. Allow enough time for the procedure.

3. You can also visit other libraries, with help from your reference librarian.

4. The *Library of Congress -- Books: Subjects* is a comprehensive subject bibliography that can lead you to books in other libraries. The *International Bibliography of Sociology* is also worth checking if you need more materials.

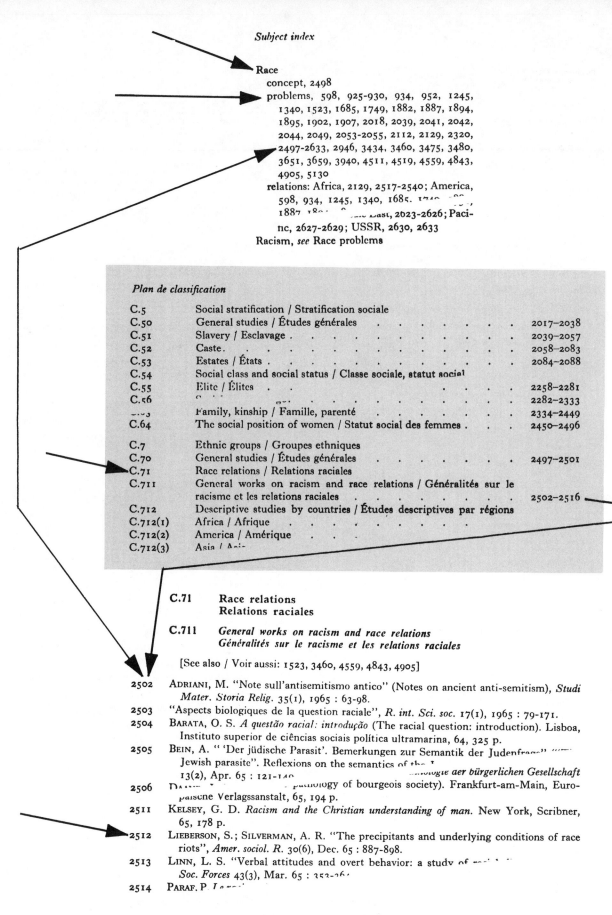

Subject index

Race
  concept, 2498
  problems, 598, 925-930, 934, 952, 1245,
    1340, 1523, 1685, 1749, 1882, 1887, 1894,
    1895, 1902, 1907, 2018, 2039, 2041, 2042,
    2044, 2049, 2053-2055, 2112, 2129, 2320,
    2497-2633, 2946, 3434, 3460, 3475, 3480,
    3651, 3659, 3940, 4511, 4519, 4559, 4843,
    4905, 5130
  relations: Africa, 2129, 2517-2540; America,
    598, 934, 1245, 1340, 1685, 1749
    1887 18   ..ast, 2023-2626; Paci-
    fic, 2627-2629; USSR, 2630, 2633
Racism, *see* Race problems

Plan de classification

C.5	Social stratification / Stratification sociale	
C.50	General studies / Études générales	2017–2038
C.51	Slavery / Esclavage	2039–2057
C.52	Caste	2058–2083
C.53	Estates / États	2084–2088
C.54	Social class and social status / Classe sociale, statut social	
C.55	Elite / Élites	2258–2281
C.56	...	2282–2333
...	Family, kinship / Famille, parenté	2334–2449
C.64	The social position of women / Statut social des femmes	2450–2496
C.7	Ethnic groups / Groupes ethniques	
C.70	General studies / Études générales	2497–2501
C.71	Race relations / Relations raciales	
C.711	General works on racism and race relations / Généralités sur le racisme et les relations raciales	2502–2516
C.712	Descriptive studies by countries / Études descriptives par régions	
C.712(1)	Africa / Afrique	
C.712(2)	America / Amérique	
C.712(3)	Asia / Asi-	

C.71 Race relations
         Relations raciales

C.711 *General works on racism and race relations*
          Généralités sur le racisme et les relations raciales

   [See also / Voir aussi: 1523, 3460, 4559, 4843, 4905]

2502 ADRIANI, M. "Note sull'antisemitismo antico" (Notes on ancient anti-semitism), *Studi Mater. Storia Relig.* 35(1), 1965 : 63-98.
2503 "Aspects biologiques de la question raciale", *R. int. Sci. soc.* 17(1), 1965 : 79-171.
2504 BARATA, O. S. *A questão racial: introdução* (The racial question: introduction). Lisboa, Instituto superior de ciências sociais política ultramarina, 64, 325 p.
2505 BEIN, A. " 'Der jüdische Parasit'. Bemerkungen zur Semantik der Judenfrage" ...
      Jewish parasite". Reflexions on the semantics of the ....ugie aer bürgerlichen Gesellschaft
2506 D.... ....pathology of bourgeois society). Frankfurt-am-Main, Euro-
      päische Verlagsanstalt, 65, 194 p.
2511 KELSEY, G. D. *Racism and the Christian understanding of man*. New York, Scribner, 65, 178 p.
2512 LIEBERSON, S.; SILVERMAN, A. R. "The precipitants and underlying conditions of race riots", *Amer. sociol. R.* 30(6), Dec. 65 : 887-898.
2513 LINN, L. S. "Verbal attitudes and overt behavior: a study of ....
      Soc. Forces 43(3), Mar. 65 : 352-361.
2514 PARAF, P. *I- ....*

Figure 35. International Bibliography of Sociology

12 A Last Word and Summary

Men are made stronger on realization that the helping hand they need is at the end of their long right arm. Sidney J. Phillips.

In conclusion, this guide has set out to teach search strategy and reference sources by means of examples. A term-paper topic, the causes of the 1965 Los Angeles Watts riot was chosen as a concrete example. Excerpts from reference sources used for the Watts riot were shown in order to demonstrate both search strategy and the use of the most important reference sources. This method was used to give you a concrete demonstration so that you could have a model for your own search. The authors hope you will pursue the following plan, outlined in this guide: choosing and narrowing your topic, using the card catalog, finding the best parts of books, evaluating books, locating current material, learning how to use government documents and statistical sources, using sociology dictionaries and guides to the literature of sociology, and finally learning how to use other libraries. When you follow this procedure, you will be using the library effectively. You may even look forward to your next term-paper assignment.

TO CHOOSE YOUR TOPIC, BEGIN BROADLY by casting
your net over a wide area. Survey possible topics in encyclopedias, handbooks, annual reviews, textbooks, and
reserve books. NARROW the possible topics on the
basis of your interests and what is available in the
library. Look for subdivisions of the broad
topics in encyclopedias, textbooks, and
reserve books. NARROW further by
using subject bibliographies and
subject subdivisions in the card
catalog. Use chapters of books
that you found under the
more relevant subject
headings.

THE CHOSEN
TOPIC

BEGIN
to look for
information
on your topic
by using the subject
heading books and trac-
ings to find the most relevant subject headings in the
card catalog. BROWSE among
the most promising books found
in the card catalog by using the indexes of the books, their bibliographies, and their footnotes. Also use the
Essay and General Literature Index to
locate parts of books. EVALUATE books
on which you plan to base your paper by
using selective bibliographies as well as indexes to book reviews and critiques. Also use
biographical sources to evaluate an author's cre-
dentials. UPDATE your bibliography by using periodical indexes, abstracts, and the *Social Sciences
Citation Index*. ENLARGE your available resources
by using government documents and statistical sources.
BROADEN your knowledge by using guides to the literature. END by surveying the realms of recorded knowledge
through the exploration of bibliographies that are arranged
by subject. Consider getting materials from other libraries.

LIBRARY KNOWLEDGE TEST

A. Directions: Use this catalog card to answer the questions below.

> **The Silverlake experiment**
>
> HV
> 9069   **Empey, LaMar Taylor, 1923–**
> E5.8   The Silverlake experiment; testing delinquency theory
>   and community intervention ₁by₁ LaMar T. Empey and
>   Steven G. Lubeck. Chicago, Aldine Pub. Co. ₁1971₁
>
>   x, 354 p. 25 cm. (Law in action)
>
>   Includes bibliographies.
>
>
>   1. Juvenile delinquency. 2. Juvenile detention homes — Case
>   studies.   I. Lubeck, Steven G., joint author. II. Title.
>
> HV9069.E58   365'.42   70-123591
> ISBN 0-202-30005-X   MARC
>
> Library of Congress   71 ₁4₁

1. Would this card be filed with other cards beginning "E," "H," "S," or "T"?
2. What is the subtitle?
3. What is the title of the series?
4. Under what other headings will cards for this book by found in the card catalog?

B. Directions: Use this excerpt from the *Readers' Guide to Periodical Literature* to answer the following questions:

5. How do you find out the full title of the periodical that carries the article, "Those Private Clubs"?
6. On what page does it appear?
7. In what volume does it appear?
8. Who is its author?
9. Under what heading will you find articles on discourtesy?
10. Does the article, "Reverse Discrimination: Has It Gone Too Far?" have any pictures?
11. Under what other subject headings will you find articles related to discrimination?

DISCOURTESY. See Courtesy
DISCOVERIES in geography
  See also
  Explorers
DISCOVERIES in science. See Science
DISCRIMINATION
  Anti-discrimination run amuck. T. Bethell. **por** Newsweek 89:11 Ja 17 '77
  Clubs: the ins and outs; private social clubs, D. M. Alpern. il Newsweek 89:18-19 Ja 10 '77
  Now, a drive to end discrimination against ugly people. il U.S. News 81:50 Ag 23 '76
  Reverse discrimination: has it gone too far? P. Oster. il U.S. News 80:26-9 Mr 29 '76
  Reverse discrimination ruled constitutional. Lib J 101:1246 Je 1 '76
  Social clubs feel the bias squeeze; preparation by Office of federal contract compliance to bar the nation's federal contractors from paying employees' dues to private social clubs whose membership policies are discriminatory. Bus W p24 Jl 19 '76
  Those private clubs. Nat R 29:79 Ja 21 '77
  Where Atlanta's Big Mules relax; barring blacks and Jews from private clubs. Time 109:11 Ja 10 '77
  See also
  Anti-Semitism
  Sex discrimination
  United Nations—Sub-commission on prevention of discrimination and protection of minorities

  Bibliography
  Dark horses (title varies) affirmative action. M. S. Evans. Nat R 28:1247 N 12 '76

The answers are at the bottom of the next page.

Answers to the Library Knowledge Test:

1. S. 2. Testing Delinquency Theory and Community Intervention. 3. Law in Action. 4. Juvenile delinquency; Juvenile detention homes — Case studies; Lubeck, Steven G., joint author; Empey, LaMar Taylor, 1923– . 5. The title is spelled out in the front of the *Readers' Guide*. You need not guess. 6. 79. 7. 29. 8. Anonymous. (Note that the author of "Antidiscrimination Run Amuck" is T. Bethell.) 9. Courtesy. 10. Yes. ("il" is the abbreviation of "illustrated.") 11. Anti-Semitism; Sex discrimination; United Nations — Sub-Commission on prevention of discrimination and protection of minorities.

Since question four has four answers and question eleven has three answers, a perfect score is 16. If you got only 10 or 11 correct, you probably need to spend time with the library guides mentioned in the Preface. If you got less than 10 correct answers, be sure to study those guides before proceeding with this book.

APPENDIX 2

BASIC REFERENCE SOURCES FOR
COURSES IN SOCIOLOGY

NOTE: This bibliography covers anthropology as well as sociology because many undergraduate departments of sociology cover the two disciplines. The first library search with any of the following course-related bibliographies will be easier if used in conjunction with Appendix 3, "Guidelines for Proceeding."

The basic work on this bibliography was completed in 1977. Then it was updated by adding new titles found in the *American Reference Books Annual* through the 1979 volume. However, time did not permit searching for post-1977 editions of older titles.

A * indicates a title described in the text.

Outline

I.   Aging; Gerontology

II.   Anthropology; Cultural Anthropology

III. Crime and Delinquency; Penology (Includes Child Abuse; Prostitution; Rape)

IV.   Ethnic groups; Race and Minority Relations
      A. Handbooks
      B. Bibliographies on Two or More Ethnic Groups
      C. American Indians; Native Americans
          1. Encyclopedias and Handbooks
          2. Bibliographies
      D. Black Americans; Negroes
          1. Encyclopedias and Handbooks
          2. Bibliographies
          3. Periodical Index
      E. Chicanos; Mexican Americans
          1. Bibliographies
          2. Directory
      F. Italians

V.   Industrial Sociology; Sociology of Occupations

VI.   Marriage and the Family; Life Cycle (Includes Abortion; Death and Dying; Divorce; Homosexuality; Sex Roles)

VII. Organizational Behavior; Community Organization

VIII. Population; Demography

IX.   Research Methods

X.   Social Change; Social Processes

XI.   Social Problems
      A. Drugs and alchohol
      B. Poverty
      C. Suicide
      D. General

XII. Social Stratification

XIII. Social Work

XIV. Sociological Theory

XV.   Sociology of Religion; Religion and Society

XVI. Urban Sociology; Cities

XVII. Women

XVIII. General
      A. Encyclopedias
      B. Handbooks
      C. Guides
      D. Dictionaries
      E. Bibliographies
          1. General
          2. Dissertations
          3. Newspapers
      F. Periodical Indexes, Abstracting Services, and Annual Reviews
      G. Statistics
      H. Biography
      I. Directories

I.   Aging; Gerontology

      A. Handbooks

          Biegel, Leonard. *The Best Years Catalogue; A*

Source Book for Older Americans. New York: Putnam, 1978. 224 pp.

Binstock, Robert H. and Ethel Shanas, eds. *Handbook of Aging and the Social Sciences.* New York: Van Nostrand Reinhold, 1977. 684 pp.

Birren, James E. and K. Warner Schaie, eds. *Handbook of the Psychology of Aging.* New York: Van Nostrand Reinhold, 1977. 787 pp.

Buckley, Joseph C. *The Retirement Handbook; A Complete Planning Guide to Your Future.* 6th ed. New York: Harper & Row, 1977. 364 pp.

Sourcebook on Aging. Chicago: Marquis Academic Media, 1977. 662 pp.

B. Bibliographies

Balkema, John B., comp. *A General Bibliography on Aging.* Washington, DC: National Council on Aging, 1972. 52 pp.

Carter, Beryl. *An Annotated Selected Bibliography for Social Work with the Aging.* New York: Council on Social Work Education, 1968. 57 pp.

Schwartz, Beverly, comp. *Aging Bibliography.* Upper Montclair, NJ: National Multimedia Center for Adult Education, Montclair State College, 1977. 84 pp.

Shock, Nathan Weatherill. *A Classified Bibliography of Gerontology and Geriatrics.* Stanford, CA: Stanford University Press, 1951. 599 pp. *Supplement, 1949--55; Supplement Two, 1956--1961,* 1963.

II. Anthropology; Cultural Anthropology

A. Encyclopedias, Handbooks, and Dictionaries

Encyclopedia of Anthropology, edited by David E. Hunter and Phillip Whitten. New York: Harper & Row, 1976. 411 pp.

Frantz, Charles. *The Student Anthropologist's Handbook; A Guide to Research, Training, and Career.* Cambridge, MA: Schenkman, 1972. 228 pp.

Murdock, George P. and others. *Outline of Cultural Materials.* 4th ed. New Haven, CT: Human Relations Area Files, 1961. 164 pp.

———. *Outline of World Cultures.* 5th ed. 1975. New Haven, CT: Human Relations Area Files, 1975. 217 pp.

Textor, Robert B., comp. *A Cross-Cultural Summary.* New Haven, CT: Human Relations Area Files, 1967.

Winick, Charles. *Dictionary of Anthropology.*

Paterson, NJ: Littlefield, Adams, 1964. 579 pp.

B. Bibliographies. (See also the section on ethnic groups)

Gutkind, Peter C.W. and John W. Webster, comp. *A Select Bibliography on Traditional and Modern Africa.* Syracuse, NY: Syracuse University, 1968. 323 pp.

Marsh, Robert Mortimer. *Comparative Sociology; A Codification of Cross-Societal Analysis.* New York: Harcourt, Brace & World, 1967. 528 pp. Bibliography, pp. 375–496.

O'Leary, Timothy J. *Ethnographic Bibliography of South America.* New Haven, CT: Human Relations Area Files, 1963. 387 pp.

Taylor, C.R.H. *A Pacific Bibliography; Printed Matter Relating to the Native Peoples of Polynesia, Melanesia and Micronesia.* 2d ed. Oxford: Clarendon, 1965. 692 pp.

U.S. Department of the Army. *Africa; A Bibliographic Survey of Literature.* Washington, DC: Government Printing Office, 1973. 545 pp.

C. Abstracting Service and Annual Review

Abstracts in Anthropology, 1970– . Westport, CT: Greenwood Periodicals, 1970– . Quarterly.

* *Annual Review of Anthropology,* 1972-- . Stanford, CA: Annual Reviews, 1972– . Annual, Preceded by: *Biennial Review of Anthropology,* 1959–1971. Stanford, CA: Stanford University Press, 1959–1972. 7 vols. Biennial.

III. Crime and Delinquency; Penology (Includes Child Abuse; Prostitution; Rape)

A. Encyclopedias and Dictionary

Branham, Vernon Carnegie and Samuel B. Kutash, eds. *Encyclopedia of Criminology.* New York: Philosophical Library, 1949. 527 pp.

Martin, Julian A. *Law Enforcement Vocabulary.* Springfield, IL: Thomas, 1973. 255 pp.

Salottolo, A. Lawrence. *Modern Police Service Encyclopedia; An Up-to-Date, Nontechnical Encyclopedic Handbook . . .* 2d ed. New York: Arco, 1973. 280 pp.

B. Bibliographies

Barnes, Dorothy L., comp. *Rape; A Bibliography 1965--1975.* Troy, NY: Whitston, 1977. 154 pp.

Bullough, Vern and others, eds. *A Bibliography of Prostitution.* New York: Garland, 1977. 419 pp.

Chambliss, William J. and Robert B. Seidman. *Sociology of the Law; A Research Bibliography.* Berkeley, CA: Glendessary, 1970. 113 pp.

Davis, Bruce L. *Criminological Bibliographies; Uniform Citations to Bibliographries, Indexes, and Review Articles of the Literature of Crime Study in the United States.* Westport, CT: Greenwood, 1978. 182 pp.

Hewitt, William H. *A Bibliography of Police Administration, Public Safety and Criminology to July 1, 1965.* Springfield, IL: Thomas, 1967. 242 pp.

Kalisch, Beatrice J. *Child Abuse and Neglect; An Annotated Bibliography.* Westport, CT: Greenwood, 1978. 535 pp.

Prostano, Emanuel T. and Martin L. Piccirillo. *Law Enforcement; A Selective Bibliography.* Littleton, CO: Libraries Unlimited, 1974. 203 pp.

Tompkins, Dorothy Louise (Campbell) Culver. *Juvenile Gangs and Street Groups; A Bibliography.* Berkeley, CA: University of California, 1966. 88 pp.

———. *The Offender; A Bibliography.* Berkeley, CA: University of California, 1963. 268 pp.

———. *Prison and the Prisoner.* Berkeley, CA: University of California, 1972. 156 pp.

———. *Sentencing the Offender; A Bibliography.* Berkeley, CA: University of California, 1971. 102 pp.

———. *White Collar Crime; A Bibliography.* Berkeley, CA: University of California, 1967. 85 pp.

Wright, Martin, ed. *Use of Criminology Literature.* Hamden, CT: Archon, 1974. 242 pp.

C. Abstracting Services

Abstracts on Crime and Juvenile Delinquency, 1968--1975. Glen Rock, NJ: Microfilming Corp. of America, 1977. 18 reels.

Crime and Delinquency Abstracts and Current Projects; An International Bibliography. Bethesda, MD: National Clearinghouse for Mental Health Information, 1963–1972.

D. Directory

American Correctional Association. *Directory of Juvenile and Adult Correctional Departments, Institutions, Agencies and Paroling Authorities, United States and Canada 1975--76.* College Park, MD: 1976. 260 pp.

E. Statistics

U.S. Federal Bureau of Investigation. *Uniform Crime Reports for the United States, 1930-- .*

IV. Ethnic Groups

A. Handbooks

Burke, Joan Martin. *Civil Rights; A Current Guide to the People, Organizations, and Events.* 2d ed. New York: Bowker, 1974. 266 pp.

The Emerging Minorities in America; A Resource Guide for Teachers. Santa Barbara, CA: American Bibliographical Center, Clio Press, 1972. 256 pp.

Keesings' Contemporary Archives. *Race Relations in the U.S.A., 1954--68.* New York: Scribner's, 1970. 280 pp.

B. Bibliographies on Two or More Ethnic Groups

Boyce, Byrl N. and Sidney Turoff. *Minority Groups and Housing; A Bibliography, 1950--1970.* Morristown, NJ: General Learning, 1972. 202 pp.

Kinton, Jack F. *American Ethnic Groups and the Revival of Cultural Pluralism; Evaluative Sourcebook for the 1970's.* 4th ed. Aurora, IL: Social Science & Sociological Resources, 1974. 206 pp.

Kitano, Harry H.L. *Asians in America; A Selected Bibliography for Use in Social Work Education.* New York: Council on Social Work Education, 1971. 79 pp.

Miller, Wayne Charles. *A Comprehensive Bibliography for the Study of American Minorities.* New York: New York University Press, 1976. 2 vols.

Wasserman, Paul and Jean Morgan. *Ethnic Information Sources of the United States; A Guide to Organizations, Agencies . . .* Detroit: Gale, 1976. 751 pp.

Wiener Library, London. *Prejudice: Racist-Religious-Nationalist; A Bibliography,* ed. by Helen Kehr. London: Institute of Contemporary History, 1971. 385 pp.

C. American Indians; Native Americans

1. Encyclopedias and Handbooks

Encyclopedia of Indians of the Americas. New York: Scholarly Press, 1974-- .

Hodge, Frederick Webb. *Handbook of American Indians North of Mexico*. Washington, DC: Government Printing Office, 1907-10. 2 vols.

Marquis, Arnold. *Guide to America's Indians; Ceremonials, Reservations and Museums*. Norman. OK: University of Oklahoma Press, 1974. 267 pp.

Reference Encyclopedia of the American Indian. 3d ed. Rye, NY: Todd, 1978. 2 vols.

Washburn, Wilcomb E., comp. *The American Indian and the United States; A Documentary History*. New York: Random House, 1973. 4 vols.

2. Bibliographies

Brennan, Jere L. *The Forgotten American -- American Indians Remembered; A Selected Bibliography for Use in Social Work Education*. New York: Council on Social Work Education, 1972. 83 pp.

Hodge, William. *A Bibliography of Contemporary North American Indians; Selected and Partially Annotated with Study Guide*. New York: Interland, 1976. 296 pp.

*Index to Literature on the American Indian, 1970-- *. San Francisco, CA: Indian Historical Society, 1972-- .

Kerri, James N. *American Indians (U.S. & Canada); A Bibliography of Contemporary Studies and Urban Research*. Monticello, IL: Council of Planning Librarians, 1973. 165 pp. *Supplement* 1974, 30 pp.

Murdock, George Peter and Timothy J. O'Leary. *Ethnographic Bibliography of North America*. 4th ed. New Haven, CT: Human Relations Area Files Press, 1975. 5 vols.

Prucha, Francis Paul. *A Bibliographical Guide to the History of Indian--White Relations in the United States*. Chicago: University of Chicago Press, 1977. 454 pp.

D. Black Americans; Negroes

1. Encyclopedias and Handbooks

Ebony. *The Negro Handbook*. Chicago: Johnson, 1966. 535 pp.

* Ploski, Harry A. and Warren Marr, comps. and eds. *The Negro Almanac; A Reference Work on the Afro American*. 3d rev. ed.; Bicentennial ed. New York: Bellwether, 1976. 1,206 pp.

Race Relations Information Center. *Directory of Afro-American Resources*, ed. by Walter Schatz. New York: Bowker, 1970. 485 pp.

Sanders, Charles L. and Linda McLean, comps. *Directory, National Black Organizations*. Harlem, NY: AFRAM, 1972. 115 pp.

Smythe, Mabel M., ed. *The Black American Reference Book*. Englewood Cliffs, NJ: Prentice-Hall, 1976. 1,026 pp.

2. Bibliographies

Davis, Lenwood. *The Black Family in Urban Areas in the United States; A Selected Bibliography of Annotated Books, Articles and Dissertations on Black Families in America*. Westport, CT: Greenwood, 1978. 132 pp.

Dunmore, Charlotte J. *Black Children and Their Families; A Bibliography*. San Francisco: R & R Research Associates, 1976. 103 pp.

Indiana University Library. *The Black Family and the Black Woman; A Bibliography*. Bloomington, IN, 1972. 107 pp.

* McPherson, James M. and others. *Blacks in America; Bibliographical Essays*. Garden City, NY: Doubleday, 1971. 430 pp.

* Miller, Elizabeth W. *The Negro in America; A Bibliography*. 2d ed. Cambridge, MA: Harvard University Press, 1970. 351 pp.

New York (City). Public Library. Schomberg Collection of Negro Literature and History. *Dictionary Catalog*. Boston: Hall, 1962. 9 vols. *Supplement*. 1st-- . 1967-- .

Porter, Dorothy Burnett. *The Negro in the United States; A Selected Bibliography*. Washington, DC: Library of Congress, 1970. 313 pp.

3. Periodical Index

* *Index to Periodical Articles By and About Blacks*. Boston: G.K. Hall, 1950-- . Annual with ten-year cumulations.

E. Chicanos; Mexican Americans

1. Bibliographies

Navarro, Eliseo. *The Chicano Community; A Selected Bibliography for Use in Social Work Education.* New York: Council on Social Work Education, 1971. 57 pp.

Pino, Frank. *Mexican Americans; A Research Bibliography.* East Lansing, MI: Michigan State University, 1974. 2 vols.

Stanford University. Center for Latin American Studies. *The Mexican American; A Selected Bibliography*, ed. by Luis G. Nogales. 2d ed. Stanford, CA: 1969. 162 pp.

2. Directory

U.S. Cabinet Committee on Opportunity for the Spanish Speaking. *Directory of Spanish Speaking Organizations in the United States.* Washington, DC: 1970. 224 pp.

F. Italians

Cordasco, Francesco and Salvatore LaGumina. *Italians in the U.S.; A Bibliography of Reports, Texts, Critical Studies and Related Materials.* New York: Oriole Editions, 1972. 137 pp.

V. Industrial Sociology; Sociology of Occupations

A. Handbooks

Handbook of Industrial and Organizational Psychology. Ed. by Marvin D. Dunnette. Chicago: Rand McNally, 1976. 1,740 pp.

U.S. Bureau of Labor Statistics. *Occupational Outlook Handbook; Employment Information on Major Occupations for Use in Guidance.* Washington, DC, 1949– . Annual.

B. Bibliographies

Forrester, Gertrude. *Occupational Literature; An Annotated Bibliography.* 1971 ed. New York: Wilson, 1971. 617 pp.

Goodman, Leonard H. *Current Career and Occupational Literature, 1973–1977.* New York: Wilson, 1978. 275 pp.

Occupation Index. Jaffrey, N.H.: Personnel

Services, 1936–68. 33 vols.

C. Periodical Index

Business Periodicals Index, 1958– . New York: Wilson, 1958– . Monthly with annual cumulations.

VI. Marriage and the Family. (See also Women)

A. Encyclopedias and Handbooks

Christensen, Harold T. *Handbook of Marriage and the Family.* Chicago: Rand McNally, 1964. 1,028 pp.

Ellis, Albert and Albert Abarbanel, eds. *Encyclopedia of Sexual Behavior.* 2d ed. New York: Hawthorn Books, 1967. 1,072 pp. (Almost identical to 1st ed.)

Mayer, Michael F. *Divorce and Annulment in the 50 States.* Rev. ed. New York: Arco Books, 1975. 96 pp.

Sussman, Marvin B. *Sourcebook in Marriage and the Family.* 4th ed. Boston: Houghton Mifflin, 1973. 389 pp.

B. Bibliographies

Aldous, John. *International Bibliography of Research in Marriage and Family 1900–1964.* Minneapolis: University of Minnesota Press, 1967. *Volume II, 1965–1972.* 1974. *Volume III, 1973 and 1974.* 1975.

Davis, Lenwood G. *The Black Family in the United States; A Selected Bibliography of Annotated Books, Articles, and Dissertations on Black Families in America.* Westport, CT: Greenwood, 1978. 132 pp.

Dollen, Charles. *Abortion in Context; A Select Bibliography.* Metuchen, NJ: Scarecrow, 1970. 150 pp.

Dunmore, Charlotte J. *Black Children and Their Families; A Bibliography.* San Francisco: R & E Research Associations, 1976. 103 pp.

Glick, Ira D. and Jay Haley. *Family Therapy and Research; An Annotated Bibliography of Articles and Books Published 1950–1970.* New York: Grune & Stratton, 1971. 280 pp.

Goode, William J. and others. *Social Systems and Family Patterns; A Propositional Inventory.* Indianapolis, IN: Bobbs–Merrill, 1971. 779 pp.

Schlesinger, Benjamin. *The Jewish Family; A Survey and Annotated Bibliography.* Toronto: University of Toronto Press, 1971.

175 pp.

─────. *Multi-Problem Family: A Review and Annotated Bibliography*. 3d ed. Toronto: University of Toronto Press, 1970. 191 pp.

─────. *The One-Parent Family; Perspectives and Annotated Bibliography*. Toronto: University of Toronto Press, 1969. 132 pp.

Straus, Murray A. *Family Measurement Techniques; Abstracts of Published Instruments, 1935–1965*. Minneapolis: University of Minnesota Press, 1969. 316 pp.

U.S. Bureau of Family Services. *Abstracts of Research and Demonstration Projects in Social Welfare and Related Fields*. Washington, DC, 1966. 249 pp.

Van Why, Elizabeth Wharton, comp. *Adoption Bibliography and Multi-Ethnic Sourcebook*. Hartford, CT: Open Door Society of Connecticut, 1977. 320 pp.

C. Directory

National Directory of Runaway Programs. 3d ed. Washington, DC: National Youth Alternatives Project, 1976. 87 pp.

Register: American Association of Marriage and Family Counselors, 1978. Claremont, CA: American Association of Marriage and Family Counselors, 1978? 355 pp.

VII. Organizational Behavior; Community Organization

A. Annual

Research Annual on Intergroup Relations. Ed. by Melvin Marvin Tumin. New York: Praeger, 1965, 1966, 1970.

B. Bibliographies

Franklin, Jerome L. *Human Resource Development in the Organization; A Guide to Information Sources*. Detroit: Gale, 1978. 175 pp.

Hare, Alexander Paul. *Handbook of Small Group Research*. New York: Free Press of Glencoe, 1962. 512 pp.

International Sociological Association. *Nature of Conflict; Studies in the Sociological Aspects of International Tensions*. Paris: UNESCO, 1957. 314 pp.

Morrison, Denton E. and Kenneth E. Hornback. *Collective Behavior; A Bibliography*. New York: Garland, 1976. 534 pp.

Rabin, Albert I. *Kibbutz Studies: A Digest of Books and Articles on the Kibbutz . . .* East Lansing, MI: Michigan State Univer-

sity Press, 1971. 124 pp.

Raven, Bertram Herbert. *A Bibliography of Publications Relating to the Small Group*. 4th ed. Los Angeles: University of California, 1969.

Requa, Eloise G. *The Developing Nations; A Guide to Information Sources Concerning Their Economic, Political, Technical and Social Problems*. Detroit: Gale Research, 1965. 339 pp.

VIII. Population; Demography

A. Handbook

Bussink, Tine and others, comps. and eds. *Sourcebook on Population, 1970–1976*. Washington, DC: Population Reference Bureau, 1976. 72 pp.

B. Bibliographies

Driver, Edwin D. *World Population Policy; An Annotated Bibliography*. Lexington, MA: Lexington Books, 1971. 1,280 pp.

Mangalam, J.J. *Human Migration; A Guide to Migration Literature in English, 1955–1962*. Lexington, KY: University of Kentucky Press, 1968. 194 pp.

Population Index. Washington, DC: Population Association of America, 1935– . Quarterly.

Texas University. Population Research Center. *International Population Census Bibliography*. Austin, TX, 1965–67. 6 vols.

C. Statistics

Ernst, Morris Leopold. *The Comparative International Almanac*. New York: Macmillan, 1967. 239 pp.

Keyfitz, Nathan and Wilhelm Flieger. *World Population; An Analysis of Vital Data*. Chicago: University of Chicago Press, 1968. 672 pp.

United Nations. *Demographic Yearbook, 1977*. 29th ed. New York, 1976. 1,024 pp.

U.S. Bureau of the Census. *Census of Population*. Washington, DC: Government Printing Office, 1790– . Decennial.

D. Directory

Trzyna, Thaddeus C., ed. *Population; An International Directory of Organizations and Information Resources*. Claremont, CA: Public Affairs Clearinghouse, 1976. 132 pp.

IX. Research Methods

A. Encyclopedias and Handbooks

Goslin, David A. *Handbook of Socialization Theory and Research*. Chicago: Rand McNally, 1969. 1,182 pp.

Miller, Delbert Charles. *Handbook of Research Design and Social Measurement*. 3d ed. New York: McKay, 1977. 518 pp.

Polansky, Norman Alburt, ed. *Social Work Research; Methods for the Helping Professions*. Rev. ed. Chicago: University of Chicago Press, 1975. 314 pp.

Ronstadt, Robert. *Art of Case Analysis; A Student Analysis Guide*. Needham, MA: Lord Publications, 1977.

B. Bibliographies

Bonjean, Charles M. *Sociological Measurement; An Inventory of Scales and Indices*. San Francisco: Chandler, 1967. 580 pp.

Frey, Frederick W. *Survey Research on Comparative Social Change; A Bibliography*. Cambridge, MA: MIT Press, 1969.

Hare, Alexander Paul. *Handbook of Small Group Research*. New York: Free Press of Glencoe, 1962. 512 pp.

Holland, Janet. *Mathematical Sociology; A Selective Annotated Bibliography*. New York: Schocken, 1970. 109 pp.

McFarland, Dalton E. *Research Methods in the Behavioral Sciences: A Selected Bibliography*. Monticello, IL: Council of Planning Librarians, 1974. 21 pp.

Survey Research and Field Techniques; A Bibliography for the Field Worker. Monticello, IL: Council of Planning Librarians, 1974. 42 pp.

X. Social Change; Social Processes

A. Dictionary

Filler, Louis. *A Dictionary of American Social Reform*. New York: Philosophical Library, 1963. 854 pp.

B. Bibliographies

Bienen, Henry. *Violence and Social Change; A Review of Current Literature*. Chicago: University of Chicago Press, 1968. 119 pp.

Brode, John. *The Process of Modernization; An Annotated Bibliography on the Socio-cultural Aspects of Development*. Cambridge, MA: Harvard University, 1969. 378 pp.

Frey, Frederick W. *Survey Research on Comparative Social Change; A Bibliography*. Cambridge, MA: MIT Press, 1969.

The Sociology of the Future; Theory, Cases and Annotated Bibliography. Edited by Wendell Bell and James A. Mau. New York: Russell Sage, 1971. Bibliography, pp. 339–454.

XI. Social Problems

A. Drugs and Alcohol

The Alcoholism Digest Annual, 1972/73– . Rockville, MD: Information Planning Associates, 1973– . Annual.

Drug Abuse Bibliography. Troy, NY: Whitston, 1970– . Annual supplement to Menditto.

Information Planning Associates. *Alcoholism Treatment and Rehabilitation; Selected Abstracts*. Rockville, MD: National Institute of Mental Health, 1972. 202 pp.

International Bibliography of Studies on Alcohol. New Brunswick, NJ: Rutgers Center of Alcohol Studies, 1966– .

Lingeman, Richard R. *Drugs from A to Z; A Dictionary*. 2d ed. New York: McGraw-Hill, 1974. 310 pp.

Menditto, Joseph. *Drugs of Addiction and Nonaddiction, Their Use and Abuse; A Comprehensive Bibliography, 1960–1969*. Troy, NY: Whitston, 1970. 315 pp.

Monroe, Margaret Ellen and Jean Stewart. *Alcohol Education for the Layman; A Bibliography*. New Brunswick, NJ: Rutgers University Press, 1959. 166 pp.

Watson, Deena D. *National Directory of Drug Abuse Treatment Programs*. Rockville, MD: National Clearinghouse for Drug Abuse Information, 1972. 381 pp.

B. Poverty

Bahr, Howard M., ed. *Disaffiliated Man: Essays and Bibliography on Skid Row, Vagrancy, and Outsiders*. Toronto: University of Toronto Press, 1970. 428 pp.

Booth, Robert E. and others. *Culturally Disadvantaged; A Bibliography and Keyword-out-of-context (KWOC) Index*. Detroit: Wayne State University Press, 1967. 803 pp.

Patti, Rino J. *Management Practice in Social Welfare: An Annotated Bibliography*. New York: Council on Social Work Education,

1976. 106 pp.

Schlesinger, Benjamin. *Poverty in Canada and the United States; Overview and an Annotated Bibliography*. Toronto: University of Toronto Press, 1966. 211 pp.

* Tompkins, Dorothy Louise (Campbell) Culver. *Poverty in the United States During the Sixties*. Berkeley, CA: University of California, 1970. 542 pp.

C. Suicide

Fareberow, Norman L. *Bibliography on Suicide and Suicide Prevention 1897--1957, 1958--1970*. Rockville, MD: National Institute of Mental Health, 1972. 126 pp.; 143 pp.

D. General

Miller, Albert Jay. *Confrontation, Conflict and Dissent; A Bibliography of a Decade of Controversy, 1960-1970*. Metuchen, NJ: Scarecrow, 1972. 567 pp.

Pinson, William. *Resource Guide to Current Social Issues*. Waco, TX: Word Books, 1968. 272 pp.

Social Alienation and Anomie; A Selected International Research Bibliography. Monticello, IL: Council of Planning Librarians, 1974. 41 pp.

Wiener Library, London. *Prejudice: Racist-Religious-Nationalist*. London: Valentine, Mitchell, 1971. 385 pp.

XII. Social Stratification

Glenn, Norval D. *Social Stratification; A Research Bibliography*. Berkeley, CA: Glendessary, 1970. 466 pp.

XIII. Social Work

A. Encyclopedia and Handbook

* *Encyclopedia of Social Work*. 17th ed. Washington, DC: National Association of Social Workers, 1977. 2 vols.

Polansky, Norman Alburt, ed. *Social Work Research; Methods for the Helping Professions*. Rev. ed. Chicago: University of Chicago Press, 1975. 314 pp.

B. Bibliographies

Carter, Beryl. *An Annotated Bibliography for Social Work with the Aging*. New York: Council on Social Work Education, 1968.

57 pp.

Li, Hong-Chan. *Social Work Education; A Bibliography*. Metuchen, NJ: Scarecrow, 1978. 341 pp.

C. Abstracting Service

Abstracts for Social Workers, 1965-- . New York: National Association of Social Workers, 1965-- . Quarterly.

D. Directory

National Handbook of Private Social Agencies, 1977--1978. Queens Village, NY: Social Science Publications, 1977.

XIV. Sociological Theory

A. Handbook

Goslin, David A. *Handbook of Socialization Theory and Research*. Chicago: Rand McNally, 1969. 1,182 pp.

XV. Sociology of Religion; Religion and Society

A. Encyclopedias

Encyclopaedia Judaica. Jerusalem: Macmillan, 1971. 16 vols.

New Catholic Encyclopedia. New York: McGraw-Hill, 1967. 15 vols. *Supplement, 1967--1974*. 1974. 520 pp.

B. Bibliographies

Berkowitz, Morris I. and J. Edmund Johnson. *Social Scientific Studies of Religion; A Bibliography*. Pittsburgh, PA: University of Pittsburgh Press, 1967. 258 pp.

Burr, Nelson R., comp. *Religion in American Life*. New York: Appleton-Century-Crofts, 1971. 171 pp.

Instituto Fe y Secularidad. *Sociologia de la Religion y Teologia/Sociology of Religion and Theology; Estudio Bibliografico/ A Bibliography*. Madrid: Editorial Cuadernos para el Diagolo, 1975. 474 pp.

XVI. Urban Sociology; Cities

A. Encyclopedias, Handbooks, and Dictionaries

Abrams, Charles. *The Language of Cities; A Glossary of Terms*. New York: Viking, 1971. 365 pp.

Encyclopedia of Urban Planning. Edited by Arnold Whittick. New York: McGraw-Hill, 1974. 1,218 pp.

Hauser, Philip Morris, ed. *Handbook for Social Research in Urban Areas.* Paris: UNESCO, 1965. 214 pp.

Leif, Irving P. *Community Power and Decision Making; An International Handbook.* Metuchen, NJ: Scarecrow, 1974. 170 pp.

Rowland, Howard S. *New York Times Guide to Federal Aid for Cities and Towns.* New York: Quadrangle Books, 1971. 1,243 pp.

B. Bibliographies

Allen, Irving Lewis. *Sociology of New Towns and New Cities; A Classified Bibliography.* Monticello, IL: Council of Planning Librarians, 1974. 19 pp.

Bell, Gwen, *Urban Environments and Human Behavior; An Annotated Bibliography.* Stroudsburg, PA: Dowden, Hutchinson & Ross, 1973. 271 pp.

Berry, Brian Joe Lobley and Allen Pred. *Central Place Studies; A Bibliography of Theory and Applications.* Philadelphia: Regional Science Research Institute, 1965. 153, 50 pp.

Branch, Melville Campbell. *Comprehensive Urban Planning; A Selective Annotated Bibliography with Related Materials.* Beverley Hills, CA: Sage, 1970. 477 pp.

Bryfogle, R. Charles. *City in Print; A Bibliography.* Morristown, NJ: General Learning Press, 1974. 324 pp. *Supplement One.* 1975. 43 pp. *Supplement Two.* 1977. 115 pp.

Hoover, Dwight W. *Cities.* New York: Bowker, 1976. 231 pp.

International Institute for Environment and Development. *Human Settlements; An Annotated Bibliography.* New York: Pergamon Press, 1976. 220 pp.

* Meyer, Jon K. *Bibliography on the Urban Crisis; The Behavioral, Psychological, and Sociological Aspects of Urban Crisis.* Chevy Chase, MD: National Institute of Mental Health, 1969. 452 pp.

Sable, Martin Howard. *Latin American Urbanization; A Guide to the Literature, Organizations, and Personnel.* Metuchen, NJ: Scarecrow, 1971. 1,077 pp.

Wallace, Rosemary H. *International Bibliography and Reference Guide on Urban Affairs.* Ramsey, NJ: Ramsey-Wallace Corp., 1966.

C. Directories

Urban Institute. *University Urban Research Centers, 1971–1972.* Edited by Grace M. Taher. 2d ed. Washington, DC, 1971. 299 pp.

Winston, Eric V.A. *Directory of Urban Affairs Information and Research Centers.* Metuchen, NJ: Scarecrow, 1970. 175 pp.

D. Statistics

International Statistical Yearbook of Large Towns. The Hague: International Statistical Institute, 1961–1972. 6 vols.

Municipal Yearbook. Washington, DC: International City Management Association, 1978. 427 pp.

U.S. Bureau of Census. *County & City Data Book, 1972.* Washington, DC: Government Printing Office, 1973. 1,020 pp.

XVII. Women (See also Marriage and the Family)

A. Encyclopedias and Handbooks

The New Woman's Survival Catalog. Edited by Susan Rennie and Kirsten Grimstad. New York: Coward, McCann & Geoghegan, 1973. 223 pp.

The New Woman's Survival Sourcebook. Edited by Kirsten Grimstad and Susan Rennie. New York: Knopf, 1975. 245 pp.

Paulsen, Kathryn and Ryan A. Kuhn. *Woman's Almanac: 12 How--To Handbooks in One.* Philadelphia: Lippincott, 1976. 624 pp.

White, William, ed. *North American Reference Encyclopedia of Women's Liberation.* Philadelphia: North American Publishing, 1972. 194 pp.

Women's Rights Almanac, 1974. Edited by Nancy Gager. Bethesda, MD: Elizabeth Cady Stanton Publishing Co., 1974. 620 pp.

B. Bibliographies

Astin, Helen S. and others. *Women; a Bibliography on Their Education and Careers.* Washington, DC: Human Service, 1971. 243 pp.

Buvinic, Mayra. *Women and World Development; an Annotated Bibliography.* Washington, DC: Overseas Development Council, 1976. 162 pp.

Een, JoAnn Delores and Marie B. Rosenberg-Dishman, comps. and eds. *Women and*

Society -- Citations 3601 to 6000; An Annotated Bibliography. Beverly Hills, CA: Sage, 1978. 277 pp. (Supplements Rosenberg.)

Hughes, Marija Matich. *The Sexual Barrier; Legal, Medical, Economic, and Social Aspects of Sex Discrimination*. Rev. ed. Washington, DC: Hughes, 1977. 843 pp.

Jacobs, Sue-Ellen. *Women in Perspective; A Guide for Cross-Cultural Studies*. Urbana, IL: University of Illinois Press, 1974. 299 pp.

Krichmar, Albert. *The Women's Movement in the Seventies; An International English-Language Bibliography*. Metuchen, NJ: Scarecrow, 1977. 875 pp.

Rihani, May and Jody Joy. *Development as If Women Mattered; An Annotated Bibliography with a Third World Focus*. Washington, DC: Overseas Development Council, 1978. 137 pp.

Rosenberg, Marie Barovic and Len V. Bergstrom, comps. and eds. *Women and Society; A Critical Review of the Literature with a Selected Annotated Bibliography*. Beverly Hills, CA: Sage, 1975. 354 pp.

Wheeler, Helen Rippier. *Womanhood Media: Current Resources about Women*. Metuchen, NJ: Scarecrow, 1972. 335 pp.

C. Biography

Ireland, Norma Olin. *Index to Women of the World from Ancient to Modern Times: Biographies and Portraits*. Westwood, MA: Faxon, 1970. 573 pp.

Notable American Women, 1607--1950, A Biographical Dictionary. Edited by Edward T. James. Cambridge, MA: Belknap Press of Harvard University Press, 1971. 3 vols.

Who's Who of American Women. 10th ed. Chicago: Marquis Who's Who, 1978. 971 pp.

D. Directories

Barrer, Myra E. *Women's Organizations & Leaders Directory, 1975--1976*. First international ed. Washington, DC: Today Publications and News Service, 1975.

E. Abstracting Service

Women Studies Abstracts. New York, 1972-- . Quarterly.

XVIII. General

A. Encyclopedias

* *Encyclopaedia of the Social Sciences*. Edited by Edwin R.A. Seligman. New York: Macmillan, 1930-4. 15 vols.

* *Encyclopedia of Social Work*. 17th ed. Washington, DC: National Association of Social Workers, 1977. 2 vols.

* *International Encyclopedia of the Social Sciences*. Edited by David L. Sills. New York: Macmillan, 1968. 17 vols.

B. Handbooks

Becker, Leonard and Clair Gustafson. *Encounter with Sociology; The Term Paper*. 2d ed. San Francisco: Boyd & Fraser, 1976. 140 pp.

Berelson, Bernard. *Human Behavior; An Inventory of Scientific Findings*. New York: Harcourt, Brace & World, 1964. 712 pp.

* Faris, Robert E.L., ed. *Handbook of Modern Sociology*. Chicago: Rand McNally, 1964. 1,088 pp.

* Lindzey, Gardner, ed. *The Handbook of Social Psychology*. 2d ed. Reading, MA: Addison-Wesley, 1968, 5 vols.

U.S. Department of Health, Education, and Welfare. *Handbook on the Programs of the U.S. Health, Education, & Welfare*. Washington, DC, 1969.

C. Guides to the Literature

Bart, Pauline. *Student Sociologist's Handbook*. 2d ed. Morristown, NJ: General Learning, 1976. 264 pp.

* Hoselitz, Berthold Frank, ed. *A Reader's Guide to the Social Sciences*. Rev. ed. New York: Free Press, 1970. 425 pp.

Mark, Charles. *Sociology of America; A Guide to Information Sources*. Detroit: Gale, 1976. 454 pp.

* Sheehy, Eugene Paul, comp. *Guide to Reference Books*. 9th ed. Chicago: American Library Association, 1976. 1,015 pp.

Walford, Albert John. *Guide to Reference Material*. 3d ed. London: Library Association, 1973-7. 3 vols. Vol. 2 is "Social and Historical Sciences, Philosophy, and Religion."

* White, Carl Milton. *Sources of Information in the Social Sciences; A Guide to the Literature*. 2d ed. Chicago: American Library Association, 1973. 702 pp.

D. Dictionaries

Clegg, Joan. *Dictionary of Social Services; Policy and Practice*. 2d ed. London: Bedford Square Press, 1977. 147 pp.

* Fairchild, Henry Pratt. *Dictionary of Sociology*. New York: Philosophical Library, 1944. 342 pp.

Gould, Julius and William L. Kolb, eds. *A Dictionary of the Social Sciences*. New York: Free Press of Glencoe, 1964. 761 pp.

* Hoult, Thomas Ford. *Dictionary of Modern Sociology*. Totowa, NJ: Littlefield, Adams, 1969. 408 pp.

* Mitchell, Geoffrey Duncan. *Dictionary of Sociology*. Chicago: Aldine, 1968. 224 pp.

Theodorson, George A. and Achilles G. Theodorson. *Modern Dictionary of Sociology*. New York: Crowell, 1969. 469 pp.

Wolman, Benjamin B. *Dictionary of Behavioral Science*. New York: Van Nostrand, Reinhold, 1973. 478 pp.

E. Bibliographies

1. General

Albert, Ethel M. *A Selected Bibliography on Values, Ethics, and Aesthetics in the Behavioral Sciences and Philosophy, 1920--1958*. Glencoe, IL: Free Press, 1959. 342 pp.

A--W Library Pathfinder. Reading, MA: Addison-Wesley, 1972-- .

Current Contents; Behavioral, Social and Educational Sciences, 1969-- . Philadelphia: Institute for Scientific Information, 1969-- . Weekly.

Current Sociology, 1952-- . Paris: UNESCO, 1952-- . Quarterly bibliography on a specific topic.

Epley, Dean G. *An Annotated Bibliography in Human Relations; The Orovilz Library Collection from 1954 to 1961*. Coral Gables, FL: University of Miami, 1962. 274 pp.

Gottlieb, David. *The Emergence of Youth Societies*. New York: Free Press, 1966. 416 pp.

* *International Bibliography of Sociology*, 1951-- . Chicago: Aldine, 1952-- . Annual.

Marsh, Robert Mortimer. *Comparative Sociology; A Codification of Cross-societal Analysis*. New York: Harcourt, Brace & World, 1967. 528 pp. Bibliography, pp. 375–496.

Padbury, Peter. *The Future; A Bibliogra-*

phy of Issues and Forecasting Techniques. Waterloo, Ont.: University of Waterloo, 1971.

Pinson, William M. *Resource Guide to Current Social Issues*. Waco, TX: Word, 1968. 292 pp.

Sussman, Marvin B., ed. *Author's Guide to Journals in Sociology & Related Fields*. New York: Haworth, 1978. 214 pp.

Wiener Library, London. *Prejudice; Racist, Religious, Nationalist; A Bibliography*. Edited by Helen Kehr. London: Institute of Contemporary History, 1971. 385 pp.

2. Dissertations

Dissertations Abstracts International. Ann Arbor, MI: Xerox University Microfilms, 1938-- .

Lunday, G. Albert. *Sociology Dissertations in American Universities, 1893--1966*. Commerce, TX: East Texas State University, 1969. 277 pp.

3. Newspapers

Ayer Directory of Publications. Philadelphia: Ayer Press, 1869-- . Annual.

From Radical Left to Extreme Right. 2d ed. Metuchen, NJ: Scarecrow, 1967–1976. 3 vols.

Wynar, Ludomyr R. and Anna T. Wynar. *Encyclopedic Directory of Ethnic Newspapers and Periodicals in the United States*. 2d ed. Littleton, CO: Libraries Unlimited, 1976. 248 pp.

F. Periodical Indexes, Abstracting Services, and Annual Reviews

Abstracts for Social Workers, 1965-- . New York: National Association of Social Workers, 1965-- . Quarterly.

Alternative Press Index, 1968-- . Baltimore, MD: Alternative Press Centre, 1970-- . Annual.

* *Annual Review of Sociology*, 1975-- . Palo Alto, CA: Annual Reviews, 1975-- . Annual.

Dissertation Abstracts International, 1938-- . Ann Arbor, MI: Xerox University Microfilms, 1938-- . Monthly.

* *Human Resources Abstracts*, 1966-- . Beverly Hills, CA: Sage, 1966-- . (Entitled *Poverty & Human Resources Abstracts* before

1975.)

Psychological Abstracts, 1927– . Washington, DC: American Psychological Association, 1927– . Monthly with semiannual cumulations.

* *Public Affairs Information Service Bulletin*, 1915– . New York, 1915– . Forty-four issues per year with cumulations five times per year and annually.

* *Readers' Guide to Periodical Literature*, 1900–. New York: Wilson, 1905– . Semi-monthly with quarterly and annual cumulations.

* *Social Sciences Citation Index*, 1972–– . Philadelphia: Institute for Scientific Information, 1973– . Three times a year with annual cumulations.

* *Social Sciences Index*, 1907– . New York: Wilson, 1916– . Quarterly with annual cumulations. Formerly *Social Sciences & Humanities Index*, 1965–1974, and *International Index*, 1907–1965.

* *Sociological Abstracts*, 1952– . San Diego, CA: American Sociological Association, 1952– . Six issues per year.

World Agricultural Economics and Rural Sociology Abstracts, 1959– . The Hague, 1965– .

G. Statistics

* *American Statistics Index . . . A Comprehensive Guide and Index to the Statistical Publications of the United States Government*. Washington, DC: Congressional Information Service, 1973–– . Annual with monthly supplements.

Gendell, Murray and Hans L. Zetterberg, eds. *A Sociological Almanac for the United States*. 2d ed. New York: Scribner's, 1964. 94 pp.

Robinson, John P. and Phillip R. Shaver. *Measures of Social Psychological Attitudes*. Rev. ed. Ann Arbor, MI: Institute for Social Research, 1973. 750 pp.

Taylor, Charles Lewis and Michael C. Hudson. *World Handbook of Political and Social Indicators*. 2d ed. New Haven, CT: Yale University Press, 1972. 443 pp.

* United Nations. Statistical Office. *Statistical Yearbook*. New York, 1949– . Annual.

U.S. Bureau of the Census. *County and City Data Book, 1972; A Statistical Abstract Supplement*. Washington, DC: 1973. 1,020 pp.

——————— . *Historical Statistics of the United States; Colonial Times to 1970*. Washington, DC, 1975. 2 vols.

* ——————— . *Statistical Abstract of the United States*. Washington, DC: Government Printing Office, 1879– . Annual.

* Wasserman, Paul, ed. *Statistics Sources; A Subject Guide to Data on Industrial, Business, Social, Educational, Financial, and Other Topics for the United States and Internationally*. 5th ed. Detroit: Gale, 1977. 976 pp.

H. Biography

* *American Men and Women of Science*. 12th ed. New York: Jaques Cattell/Bowker, 1973. Two volumes are subtitled "The Social and Behavioral Sciences."

* American Sociological Association. *Directory*. New York, 1950– . Triennial.

* *Biography Index; A Cumulative Index to Biographical Material in Books and Magazines*, 1946– . New York: Wilson, 1947– . Quarterly with annual and three-year cumulations.

Dictionary of American Biography. New York: Scribner's, 1928–– . Has articles on deceased persons who lived in the United States.

Dictionary of National Biography. New York: Macmillan, 1908– . Has articles on deceased Britishers.

* *International Who's Who*. London: Europa, 1935– .

* *New York Times Obituary Index, 1858–1968*. New York: New York Times, 1970. 1,136 pp.

Notable American Women, 1607–1950; A Biographical Dictionary. Edited by Edward T. James. Cambridge, MA: Belknap Press of Harvard University Press, 1971. 3 vols.

* *Who's Who; An Annual Biographical Dictionary*. London: Black, 1849– . Annual.

* *Who's Who in America; A Biographical Dictionary of Notable Living Men and Women*. Chicago: Marquis, 1899– . Biennial.

Who's Who in the East; A Biographical Dictionary of Noteworthy Men and Women of the Middle Atlantic and Northeastern States and Canada. Chicago: Marquis, 1943– . Biennial.

Who's Who in the Midwest; A Biographical Dictionary of Noteworthy Men and Women of the Central and Midwestern States. Chicago: Marquis, 1949– . Biennial.

Who's Who in the South and Southwest; A Biographical Dictionary of Noteworthy Men and Women of the Southern and Southwestern States. Chicago: Marquis, 1950– . Biennial.

Who's Who in the West; A Biographical Dictionary of Noteworthy Men and Women of the Pacific Coastal and Western States. Chicago: Marquis, 1949– . Biennial.

* *Who's Who in the World.* Chicago: Marquis, 1970– .

Who's Who of American Women. Chicago: Marquis, 1959– . Biennial.

I. Directories

American Sociological Association. *Guide to Graduate Departments of Sociology, 1977.* Washington, DC: 1976? 304 pp.

Child Welfare League of America. *Directory of Member Agencies.* 44th ed. New York, 1977.

Christiano, David, ed. *Human Rights Organizations and Periodicals Directory, 1977.* Berkeley, CA: Meiklejohn Civil Liberties Institute, 1977. 147 pp.

Directory of Agencies: U.S. Voluntary, International Voluntary, Intergovernmental. Washington, DC: National Association of Social Workers, 1975. 100 pp.

Encyclopedia of Associations. 13th ed. Detroit: Gale, 1979. 1,477 pp. Supplements are entitled New Associations and Projects.

Haimes, Norma. *Helping Others; A Guide to Selected Social Services Agencies and Occupations.* New York: John Day, 1974. 208 pp.

National Directory of Private Social Agencies, 1977--1978. Queens Village, NY: Social Science Publications, 1977. Monthly supplements.

Research Centers Directory. 5th ed. Detroit: Gale, 1975. 1,039 pp.

Social Service Organizations. Edited by Peter Romanofsky. Westport, CT: Greenwood, 1978. 2 vols.

Urban Institute. *University Urban Research Centers, 1971--1972.* Edited by Grace M. Taher. 2d ed. Washington, DC, 1971. 299 pp.

Winston, Eric V.A., comp. *Directory of Urban Affairs Information and Research Centers.* Metuchen, NJ: Scarecrow, 1970. 175 pp.

Wynar, Ludomyr Roman. *Encyclopedic Directory of Ethnic Organizations in the United States.* Littleton, CO: Libraries Unlimited, 1975. 414 pp.

GUIDELINES FOR PROCEEDING

The questions below are designed to lead a student through a library search on a term paper topic in sociology. Some questions will lead to valuable materials; others will lead to dead ends. The questions pretty much follow the chapters in this book, so if any questions need clarification, refer back to the appropriate chapter.

1. My tentative topic or topics (Chapter 1):

2. Choosing a more precise topic.

    a. What encyclopedias, handbooks, and annual reviews listed in Appendix 2 are most useful?

    b. Is my topic interdisciplinary? If so, what encyclopedias, handbooks, and annual reviews does the reference librarian recommend?

    c. What textbooks and reserve books are most useful?

3. Narrowing the topic. (Chapter 2)

    a. What narrowing is suggested by the above encyclopedias, handbooks, annual reviews, textbooks, and reserve books?

    b. What narrowing is suggested by bibliographies? (Check those in Appendix 2 as well as those found in the card catalog under the subject subdivision, " – Bibliography." Also check with your reference librarian.)

4. Communicating with the card catalog. (Chapter 3)

    a. What subject heading(s) in the subject heading books most precisely describe my topic?

    b. What related headings are suggested by "sa" and "xx" in the subject heading books and by "see also" references in the card catalog?

    c. When I check the above headings in the card catalog, what books appear most useful?

5. Evaluating books. (Chapter 5)

    a. On what books am I basing my paper?

    b. Have they appeared on selective bibliographies?

    c. Have they been favorably reviewed? Have reviewers disagreed with any important facts or interpretations? (Check *Book Review Digest, Book Review Index*, and the reference librarian.)

    d. If I find no information for *b* and *c* above, do any of the following indicate whether the author is an authority? American Sociological Association. *Directory? American Men and Women of Science? Biography Index?*

6. Collecting current information. This is especially important for topics of recent controversy. (Chapter 6)

    a. What useful articles are cited in the *Social Sciences Index?*

    b. In *Sociological Abstracts?*

    c. In the *Social Sciences Citation Index?*

7. Government documents. (Chapter 7)

    Does the *Monthly Catalog* cite any documents that bear on my topic?

8. Statistical sources. (Chapter 8)

    Can I support my generalizations with statistics from:

    a. *Statistical Abstract of the United States?*

    b. *American Statistics Index?*

    c. Any other sources described in Chapter 8?

9. Using guides to the literature of sociology, in case my bibliography is weak. (Chapter 10)

a. What useful sources are cited in *Sources of Information in the Social Sciences*?

b. In *A Reader's Guide to the Social Sciences*?

10. Using comprehensive bibliographies, if my bibliography is still weak. (Chapter 11)

    a. What useful books are cited in *Library of Congress Catalog -- Books: Subjects*?

b. In *International Bibliography of Sociology*?

11. Using other libraries. (Chapter 11)

    a. If important books and articles are not in my library, do I have time to request interlibrary loans or photocopies?

    b. Shall I visit another library?

Index of Titles

Note: This index includes only the *reference* sources treated in the twelve chapters. It excludes non-reference books and works cited only in the appendices.

American Men and Women of Science 24
American Statistics Index 36, 38
Annual Review of Anthropology 4
Annual Review of Psychology 4
Annual Review of Sociology 4, 6
Bibliography on the Urban Crisis 9, 10
Biennial Review of Anthropology 4
Biography Index 24
Black Information Index 42
Blacks in America; Bibliographical Essays 11-12, 13, 21, 22
Book Review Digest 21
Book Review Index 21, 23
C.R.I.S.; The Combined Retrospective Index Set to Journals in Sociology, 1895-1974 28, 29
Concise Guide to Library Research 15
Contemporary Authors 25
County and City Data Book 36
Current Book Review Citations 21, 23
Demographic Yearbook 36
Dictionary of Modern Sociology 39
Dictionary of Sociology 39, 40
Directory (American Sociological Association) 24
Education Index 23
Elsevier's Dictionary of Criminal Sciences 39
Encyclopedia of the Social Sciences 2
Encyclopedia of Social Work 2
Essay and General Literature Index 20
Guide to Reference Books 42
Handbook of Modern Sociology 4, 5
Handbook of Social Psychology 4
Handbook of Socialization Theory and Research 4
Human Resources Abstracts 28
Humanities Index 23
Index to Legal Periodicals 23
Index to Periodical Articles By and About Blacks 28
Index to Religious Periodical Literature see Religion Index One: Periodicals

International Bibliography of Sociology 44, 46
International Encyclopedia of the Social Sciences 2, 3
International Index 26, 28
International Who's Who 25
Library of Congress Catalog – Books: Subjects; A Cumulative List of Works Represented by Library of Congress Printed Cards 44, 45
Library of Congress Subject Headings 16
Monthly Catalog of United States Government Publications 34-35
Multilingual Demographic Dictionary 39
National Union Catalog of the Library of Congress 44
The Negro Almanac 9-10
The Negro in America; A Bibliography 11, 12
New Serial Titles 44
New York Times Index 30, 32
New York Times Obituary Index, 1858-1968 25
Poverty in the United States During the Sixties; A Bibliography 10
Poverty Studies in the Sixties; A Selected, Annotated Bibliography 10, 11
Public Affairs Information Service. Bulletin 27, 28
Readers' Guide to Periodical Literature 23, 24, 26
A Reader's Guide to the Social Sciences 42
Religion Index One: Periodicals 23
Social Sciences & Humanities Index 26
Social Sciences Citation Index 21, 23, 28, 30, 31
Social Sciences Index 23, 26, 27, 32
Sociological Abstracts 26, 27, 31, 32
Sources of Information in the Social Sciences; A Guide to the Literature 41, 42
Statistical Abstract of the United States 36, 37
Statistical Yearbook 36
Statistics Sources 36
Student Sociologist's Handbook 42
Union List of Serials 44
Who Was Who 25
Who Was Who in America 25
Who's Who 25
Who's Who in America 25
Who's Who in the World 25

Notes

Notes

Notes